THE UNIVERSITY OF CHICAGO
ORIENTAL INSTITUTE PUBLICATIONS

SENNACHERIB'S AQUEDUCT AT JERWAN

THE UNIVERSITY OF CHICAGO PRESS
CHICAGO, ILLINOIS

THE BAKER & TAYLOR COMPANY
NEW YORK

THE CAMBRIDGE UNIVERSITY PRESS
LONDON

THE MARUZEN-KABUSHIKI-KAISHA
TOKYO, OSAKA, KYOTO, FUKUOKA, SENDAI

THE COMMERCIAL PRESS, LIMITED
SHANGHAI

Royal Air Force Official

THE JERWAN AQUEDUCT. AIR VIEW

THE UNIVERSITY OF CHICAGO
ORIENTAL INSTITUTE PUBLICATIONS
VOLUME XXIV

SENNACHERIB'S AQUEDUCT AT JERWAN

By

THORKILD JACOBSEN *and* SETON LLOYD

WITH A PREFACE BY HENRI FRANKFORT

THE UNIVERSITY OF CHICAGO PRESS
CHICAGO, ILLINOIS

COMPOSED AND PRINTED BY THE UNIVERSITY OF CHICAGO PRESS
CHICAGO, ILLINOIS, U.S.A.

PREFACE

It so happens that the first final publication of work undertaken by the Iraq Expedition refers neither to one of the sites for which the Oriental Institute holds a somewhat permanent concession nor to a task carried out by the expedition as a whole. The aqueduct at Jerwan—identified by Dr. Jacobsen at the end of the 1931/32 season—was explored by the two authors of this volume in March and April, 1933, on the strength of a sounding permit of four weeks' validity. Mrs. Rigmor Jacobsen was responsible for the photography. It was only by dint of a sustained and strenuous effort that the excavation was completed within the stipulated period. In March, 1934, the same party went up to Ḫines in the Gomel gorge and explored the head of the Bavian-Khosr canal, which links up with the aqueduct at Jerwan. This volume had then already been written, except for its last chapter.

The discoveries at Jerwan have a twofold significance. In the first place they reveal a type of structure which nowhere else survives from pre-Roman times. Mr. Lloyd's detailed essay, which forms the second chapter of the present volume, does full justice to this side of the discovery. Secondly, fresh light is thrown on the civic works undertaken by Sennacherib; in fact, much of the great Bavian inscription only now becomes intelligible. Dr. Jacobsen has followed up his new information to such an extent that the ancient geography of the region involved and the sequence in which the waterworks were carried out have become well established. In doing so he has thrown some curious sidelights on the character of Sennacherib. When he plausibly suggests that the revolutionary town-planning of Sargon at Khorsabad influenced his son's projects, the work at Jerwan is linked with the main task of our expedition in Assyria.

There is in several respects a close connection between the present-day population of our part of Iraq and that of the ancient world with which we are dealing. In chapter iv it is related how the Yezidis were discovered to have preserved a tradition which accounts for the use of the aqueduct and the layout of the watercourse and which survived the actual functioning of the system for more than two thousand years. Nor is this astonishing fact an isolated phenomenon. At Khorsabad we have witnessed a rain charm representing dramatically the death and resurrection of a male figure and the wailing of a female one, with obvious references to fertility rites.[1] There cannot be the slightest doubt that that dance reflects a mythology rooted in the oldest stratum of Western Asiatic beliefs of which we have knowledge. Though the name of Tammuz is lost in this case, it survives in that of the god of the Yezidis, Melek (i.e., King) Taʿuz. And at the Yezidi shrine of Shaikh Adi (Pls. I–II) we have seen the red anemones, Adonis' flower, stuck above the doors in spring.

Elsewhere I have tried to show that in certain remote regions of East Africa groups of men survive who preserve in their physique and in their culture many features characteristic of the population which preceded the rise of pharaonic civilization.[2] A similar relationship seems to exist between the modern population of northeastern Iraq and the ancient inhabitants of that region, for the cultural parallels are accompanied by a resemblance in physical type which is not less striking. Plates III–IV show one of our Yezidi workmen and a modern Assyrian

[1] *Iraq* I (1934) 137–45.

[2] "Modern Survivors from Punt," *Studies Presented to F. Ll. Griffith* (London, 1932) pp. 445–53.

(Nestorian) priest who could have served as prototypes for figures on ancient Assyrian reliefs. They represent the mountaineer element in the ancient Assyrian population which may perhaps be called Hurrian. The modern representatives have only recently been measured and described;[3] their cephalic index is about 83. Farther to the north (and therefore out of the reach of our photographer) live mountaineers with an even more extreme brachycephalic development (86) and characterized by sharp, hooked noses. This Armenian type is better known not only in modern anthropological literature but also from ancient Egyptian monuments where Hittites are depicted. Its influence on the Assyrian people is indirect, due to a probably Syrian, Semitic-speaking element; it can be illustrated by the modern example of the four figures on the left in Plate V*A*. That picture, showing a group of Arab workmen, illustrates the physical difference between the Semites of ancient Assyria and those of ancient Babylonia. The latter are represented by the two figures on the right, who are of pure Bedawi type, dolichocephalic "Mediterraneans" with straight, short nose slightly rounded at the point, such as both Naramsin and Hammurabi possess in the reliefs. Contenau has graphically described this as "légèrement 'en pied de marmite' "[4] without, however, referring to the modern representatives described by F. von Luschan.[5] But the fleshy hooked nose seen in the reliefs of the ancient Assyrian Semites and the brachycephaly observable in their modern representatives (Pl. V*A*, the four figures on the left) show that a considerable admixture with "Armenoids" has taken place. An ivory from the tomb of King "Qa," of the first Egyptian dynasty, which pictures most probably a Syrian captive,[6] suggests that the mixture took place in North Syria before the end of the fourth millennium B.C.

Though it is obvious that our archeological expedition cannot devote itself to anthropological research, the first requirement of which is a prolonged and uninterrupted stay among the population concerned, the foregoing remarks should establish the importance of the anthropological material which came to our notice while we were working in this region.

It remains to thank the authorities who assisted us during the excavations at Jerwan. First we should record the friendly co-operation received throughout from Tahsin Bey Askari, mutasarrif of Mosul Liwa, and from Major W. C. F. Wilson, administrative inspector. The establishment of quarters at ᶜAin Sifni was made possible by the courtesy of Michael Effendi Tessy, kaimakam of Shaikhan, and Abdullah Effendi, chief of police at ᶜAin Sifni. The interest of the Kaimakam in the progress of the work and in the well-being of the expedition proved on various occasions an invaluable asset. Dr. Petros de Baz assisted us in maintaining the health of the little party as well as in establishing contact with certain natives whose folklore was an object of interest both to him and to ourselves. We wish to express our gratitude to these gentlemen for the friendly assistance which they granted us and which materially furthered the completion of the work.

HENRI FRANKFORT

TELL ASMAR
December, 1934

[3] C. U. Ariëns Kappers, *An Introduction to the Anthropology of the Near East in Ancient and Recent Times* (Amsterdam, 1934) chaps. ii, iii, and v.

[4] G. Contenau, *Manuel d'archéologie orientale* I (Paris, 1927) 102.

[5] In *Journal of the Royal Anthropological Institute* XLI (1911) 235.

[6] W. M. F. Petrie, *The Royal Tombs of the First Dynasty* (London, 1900) Pls. XII 12–13 and XVIII 30.

TABLE OF CONTENTS

LIST OF ILLUSTRATIONS

PLATES

TEXT FIGURES

I

OUR FIRST VISIT TO JERWAN

In April, 1932, while the writer was spending some weeks in Khorsabad his attention was called to a curious story told by one of the workmen. This man had found work the previous summer among the foothills of the mountains in a small village where, he affirmed, not only had inscribed stones been used in building the houses but others also inscribed were placed as seats outside the doors. We were tempted at first to be incredulous, owing to the number of such stories which had previously been brought to us and on investigation had resulted in sad disillusionment. Sometimes these had spoken of subterranean chambers lined with marble slabs, and often of inscriptions. But the former usually proved to be natural formations, and the latter to be cracks on the face of a stone. This time, however, the story-teller went so far as to produce a sketch he had made of various signs from the inscriptions. This at once made it clear that his story was genuine, since the characters were definitely cuneiform. Accordingly on the following day I set out in search of the village with the man, Hussein ᶜAli of Faddhiliyah, as guide.

Leaving Khorsabad in the morning we took the main road to ᶜAin Sifni (see Fig. 9), where we turned right, following a mule track which ran among the foothills. The track crossed several wadies, but as it had been a rather dry spring they presented no serious difficulties. About midday we reached our destination. A turn of the road showed us a long narrow valley descending from the mountains behind. Across this valley like a barrier stretched a low wall of stone so completely covered with grass that it was only recognizable as such in a few places where the stones projected above the turf. In the center of this wall was a breach through which flowed a small brook; and on the left bank of the latter, partly overlapping the stone structure, appeared a cluster of about eighteen mud houses which constituted the village of Jerwan.

On our arrival the village came suddenly to life, and we were met by the mukhtar, ᶜAli, an impressive old man of pure Yezidi type, who showed us round the place. The houses (e.g. Pl. V*B*) were indeed built partly of mud brick and partly of pieces of hewn stones many of which bore cuneiform characters. When the inscriptions on these wall stones had been compared and put together, they proved to be fragments of various copies of a single short inscription (*A*; see p. 19) recording the name and titles of Sennacherib. But there were traces of still another inscription. In front of the gate to the mukhtar's house was a bench formed of a row of stone blocks, each about 52×52×52 centimeters in size, two of which were inscribed. However, whereas the signs on the stones in the walls had been only about 6 centimeters high, the signs on the bench blocks measured 10 centimeters. Each block had four lines of writing, but the signs were so large that there were only three or four of them on each line. It was therefore impossible to form any opinion as to the content of the inscription to which they belonged.

When questioned as to where these inscribed blocks had come from, the mukhtar answered that together with the stones in the walls they had been taken from the old stone dam against which the village was built. He admitted the existence of other, similar stones still in place, but said they were now covered with turf. Later, however, he offered to have some villagers clear them; and while this work was in progress we followed him to the village guestroom, where a delicious meal of curds, honey, and the crisp bread baked by the Yezidis had been prepared for us. During the meal conversation flagged a little, partly because the mukhtar and the villagers knew only a few words of Arabic and partly because of our preoccupation with the art of balancing curds and honey on pieces of bread which served temporarily as spoons. It was therefore not until later, when pipes had been lighted and coffee brought around, that we were able to obtain information concerning the curious stone wall behind the village. Hussein, who spoke the Yezidi dialect and Arabic equally well, proved a rather skilful interpreter. With his help we learned how once long ago the whole of the plain below Jerwan had been a great lake and how a man by the name of Suliman Titi had built an enormous stone dam and stemmed the water so that the lake dried up and its bottom became a fertile plain.

In return for this story we on our side had to tell what the inscriptions contained and who Sennacherib was—how he had reigned in Kuyunjik and how he was the son of the king who had built at Khorsabad. In the midst of a lively discussion as to whether the Sennacherib of the inscriptions might perhaps be the same as Suliman Titi, a boy came in to say that the stones which lay "side by side" were now uncovered. Following him to the end of the village, we found that a hole had been dug beside one of the houses, disclosing a stone surface which carried a four-line inscription. The signs at the ends of the lines were clear, but the beginnings seemed to be under the house where a thick deposit of salt made them illegible. The legible part, however, was sufficiently exciting; it read as follows:

> Its [. . . .] to it I added. [. . . .] I caused to be dug
> [. . . .] . Over deep-cut ravines
> [. . . .] white I spanned a bridge.
> [. . . .] I caused to pass over upon it.

Even these bits were enough to make it fairly certain that the inscription recorded the construction of a bridge and that the colossal stone structure before us, more than 300 meters long from end to end, was thus not a dam, as local tradition had seemed to indicate, but a bridge—the oldest bridge, in fact, of which remains are still extant.[1] For the bridge discovered

[1] As far as I know, the earliest bridge mentioned in cuneiform literature is one built in Susa by the ruler Addapakshu at the time of the first dynasty of Babylon. The inscription recording it ("Mémoires de la Délégation en Perse" II [1900] Pl. 15, No. 5, and IV [1902] Pl. 1, No. 8; Thureau-Dangin, *Die sumerischen und akkadischen Königsinschriften* [Leipzig, 1907] pp. 182–83) was written on bricks, and thus it would seem to have been constructed of that material.

The next bridge a record of which is extant is a boat-bridge pictured on one of the bronze bands from the gates of Shalmaneser III at Tell Balawat. This bridge seems to have been a temporary structure only. See British Museum, *A Guide to the Babylonian and Assyrian Antiquities*, 3d ed. (London, 1922) Pl. XXI.

Later Tiglathpileser III mentions that during a campaign he cut down trees; he continues: *ti-tur-ra-a-ti* (var. *-te*) *a-na me-ti-iq um-ma-na-a-te-i̯a*^{meš} *lu ú-ṭí-ib* (Rawlinson, *The Cuneiform Inscriptions of Western Asia* I [London, 1861] 12 iv 69 f.), "verily I improved the bridges for the passing of my troops." This passage, however, appears to refer only to repair of bridges already existing.

Sargon II of Assyria does not in his annals mention any bridges which he himself built, for all obstacles encountered by his warriors are miraculously surmounted; they "fly across them like birds." He tells, however, how Merodachbaladan, who had fortified his camp with a water-filled ditch 99 m. wide, "broke off the bridges" (*ú-bat-ti-qa ti-tur-re*) when Sargon approached (Hugo Winckler, *Die Keilschrifttexte Sargons* [Leipzig, 1889] No. 73:128 f.). These bridges must have been of considerable length and were probably boat-bridges.

The first bridge built of bricks after that of Addapakshu is that which Sennacherib built in Nineveh across the Khosr. He says (see p. 21): "A bridge of baked bricks (and) white stone blocks I spanned (*lit.*, caused to step) for my royal passing." No remnants of this bridge have yet been found.

Next to the Nineveh bridge in age comes Sennacherib's bridge—actually an aqueduct—at Jerwan (the subject of this volume). A later aqueduct is pictured on a slab from the palace of Ashurbanipal (British Museum, *op. cit.* p. 50, No. 92; see also Valentin Müller in *Reallexikon der Assyriologie* I [Berlin and Leipzig, 1932] 124–25 and the literature quoted there). The latter is built of stone blocks and to judge from the picture had corbeled arches.

Of Babylonian bridges we know, besides those of Merodachbaladan mentioned above, a bridge built by Nebuchadnezzar II in Babylon: *i-na ai̯-*[*i-bur-ša-bu-um*] *su-li-e* [*bāb-ili*^{ki}] *a-na ma-aš-da-ḫu* [*bēlu rabū* ^{d}*marduk*] *ti-tu-ur-ru* [*palgi ak-ṣur*] ^{iṣ}*miskannu* . . . . ^{iṣ}*erini* . . . . , "in Ai[burshabu], the (main) street [of Babylon], [I constructed] a bridge for the

by Koldewey in Babylon dates from the Neo-Babylonian period, whereas this—as indicated by Sennacherib's name upon the stones—would be considerably older. Most important of all, the state of the ruins gave every hope that this bridge would be exceptionally well preserved, far better than the bridge at Babylon, of which only the foundations of the piers have survived.

The startling information thus supplied by the inscription was ample recompense for any unpleasantness involved in copying it. The place where the inscription was found evidently served the villagers as a dunghill, and in the scorching sun the hole—half full of filthy water—was anything but inviting. Nor did the actual process of copying pass off as quietly as might have been expected. Tired of watching, some of the onlookers had discovered the tail of a snake projecting from the wall of the neighboring house. Around this they quietly tied a piece of string, and by pulling hard four or five men endeavored to extract the snake from the wall. The snake, which later proved to be over a meter long, put up a good fight; and when in the end it came away men and snake together fell backward into the hole. By a sheer miracle no one was bitten, and after the snake had been duly killed we were able to continue copying. When our copy was finished we photographed the inscriptions and, by pacing out the distances, made a rough sketch of the bridge. Then we bade the mukhtar and the villagers goodbye and returned to Khorsabad.

In a country like Iraq, which for more than a century has been a center of archeological exploration, it could hardly be expected that a monument of such size as the bridge at Jerwan should have escaped notice completely. Thus it was really not altogether unexpected that any illusion we were under concerning our priority in discovering Jerwan was shattered upon looking through the pertinent literature before writing this chapter.

The first European to visit the village and describe the ruins would seem to have been Layard; for after describing the rock sculptures at Bavian he adds: "The remains of a well-built raised causeway of stone, leading to Bavian from the city of Nineveh, may still be traced across the plain to the east of the Gebel Makloub."[2] This description seemed to fit the remains of the bridge as it looked before our excavation, with the stone pavement of the canal

---

procession [of the great lord Marduk]; mulberry wood, ... , cedar wood . . . . ." See S. Langdon, *Die neubabylonischen Königsinschriften* (Leipzig, 1912) p. 160, line 60; cf. p. 88, col. ii 5. The bridge here referred to led across the Libilḫegalla canal and was apparently built of wood, for the various sorts of wood mentioned in the text were evidently used in its construction.

The Euphrates bridge found by Koldewey dated from somewhat before the time of Nebuchadnezzar. This was 115 m. long and about 6 m. wide (according to Unger, cited below, based on width of landward pier at west end; Wetzel's reconstruction in his Pl. 51, showing only 1–1.40 m., seems to me less probable). It rested on 6 piers each 21 m. long and 9 m. wide. These piers were built of baked bricks and were shaped like boats. The superstructure seems to have consisted of wood. See F. Wetzel, *Die Stadtmauern von Babylon* (48. Wissenschaftliche Veröffentlichung der Deutschen Orient-Gesellschaft [1930]) pp. 55 f.

These and other passages relating to bridges may be found in Eckhard Unger, *Babylon* (Berlin and Leipzig, 1931) pp. 116–18, and in the literature quoted there.

As shown by this short summary, more than one type of bridge was familiar to Assyrian-Babylonian culture. We find first the boat-bridge, consisting of pontoons anchored in the stream with a simple superstructure of wood laid across from boat to boat. Although we know this type of bridge for certain from an Assyrian rendering only, it seems likely that its origin was in Babylonia, for the materials used in its construction are such as could be procured there. The other underlying type, the bridge with corbeled arches, illustrated by Ashurbanipal's aqueduct, must have originated in a mountainous country where stones were easily obtainable—i.e., either in Assyria or in Elam. These two original types, however, influenced each other, so that features of both came to be combined. E.g. the Euphrates bridge found by Koldewey at Babylon had fixed piers in the middle of the stream as does the corbeled-arch type; but these piers were built in the shape of boats, and the wooden superstructure of the boat-bridge was retained. The Jerwan aqueduct also shows influences from both types; generally speaking, it belongs to the corbeled-arch type, but the piers are boat-shaped and the flanking buttresses, which have no structural function, may perhaps have been derived from such piers. If so, the fact that the bridge buttresses are square, not rounded like pontoons, could be due to the secondary influence of temple and fortress architecture.

[2] A. H. Layard, *Discoveries in the Ruins of Nineveh and Babylon* (London, 1853) p. 216.

bed showing in places along its top; so, in spite of the words "to the east of the Gebel Makloub"—Jerwan is situated north or north-northwest of this range—we may assume that it was to this bridge that he was referring.

The next to visit Jerwan was L. W. King, who passed by it on his way to Bavian in 1904 and photographed the ruins. King shared Layard's opinion that the remains were those of a road. He rightly assigned them to Sennacherib on the basis of inscriptions which he found in the village of Mahad situated about three miles southeast of Jerwan as the crow flies. King's account of his visit is found in a letter written to Eduard Meyer in 1914 and published later by Bachmann: "I give a photograph of the paved causeway on the way to Bavian, which should be traced out and planned. At Mahad, a neighbouring village, I found several inscribed stones built into the houses, two of which bore Sennacherib's name. These probably came from the causeway, which has been used locally as a quarry for building material."[3] This letter was written because the Deutsche Orient-Gesellschaft had planned a reinvestigation of the rock sculptures at Maltai and Bavian, which was carried out a few months later (May, 1914) by Bachmann. On the instigation of King this investigation included Jerwan also.

Before describing the results of Bachmann's investigation, however, we should mention that in 1908 Olmstead seems to have passed by Jerwan. Describing his approach to the gorge of Bavian, he writes: "Riding across the rolling plain and following up the line of that Gomel River which preserves the name of the Gau Gamela where Alexander won the world, we pass the raised stone track along which went the canal."[4] Although he does not mention any detail which might have helped to locate the place he has in mind, there can be little doubt that it is the bridge at Jerwan; for this is the only place I know of where the canal can be said to run on a raised stone track. There is, in spite of the inconclusive topography, special reason to mention Olmstead's account, as he is the only one of the earlier visitors who connected the ruins with a canal.

While Layard, King, and Olmstead had contented themselves with giving only a short description of the ruins, Bachmann made a regular survey and recorded the ruins as thoroughly as was possible without actual digging.[5] He gives a plan and two sections, to which he adds a short description of the masonry, noting the difference in size between the pavement stones on top and the bigger stones below. He describes the layer of concrete also. A few of his statements, for example that the masonry comes out in steps at the bottom, are not correct; but such mistakes were almost unavoidable, since he could observe it in only a few places where it was not covered with turf and was compelled to generalize from these.[6]

As to the explanation of the ruins, Bachmann rejects Layard's theory of a raised causeway from Bavian to Nineveh, partly because of the direction, which is almost due east–west, and the "räumlich beschränkte Ausdehnung des Ganzen"[7] and partly because, as he rightly remarks, "das Bauwerk hat zudem auf eng begrenzter Stelle noch heute im Ruinenzustande eine solche Mächtigkeit, dass die obige Deutung wohl einer nur sehr flüchtigen Besichtigung zuzuschreiben ist."[8] Instead, he puts forward the theory that the structure was a dam, which by closing the valley behind converted it into a natural reservoir where water would be stored for irrigation purposes: "Das Bauwerk stellt sich dar als Rest eines ausgedehnten steinernen

[3] W. Bachmann, *Felsreliefs in Assyrien* (52. Wissenschaftliche Veröffentlichung der Deutschen Orient-Gesellschaft [1927]) p. vi.

[4] A. T. Olmstead, *History of Assyria* (New York and London, 1923) p. 332.

[5] Bachmann, *op. cit.* pp. 32–33 and Pl. 33.

[6] *Ibid.* p. 32: "Verfall und starke Bewachsung erlaubten kein absolut genaues Aufnehmen."

[7] *Ibid.* [8] *Ibid.*

Dammes, der ein Becken von etwa 3 km Länge und 1 km grösster Breite in den Gebirgsausläufern dort abschliesst, wo sich die begrenzenden Höhen am meisten nähern und die günstigste Lage für einen Staudamm geben. Ein kleiner Bach fliesst noch heute durch diese Senke, der, wie man erkennen kann, zuzeiten reichliche Hochwassermengen führt. Der Damm bildete so eine künstliche Talsperre, die dazu diente, grössere Wassermengen zur Bewässerung der anschliessenden Ebene aufzuspeichern."[9]

We have quoted Bachmann's theory at some length, partly because as an explanation of the data then available it was very attractive indeed, partly also because we believe it to be at the bottom of the local tradition told us by the mukhtar on our first visit to Jerwan.[10] Since that tradition is almost identical with Bachmann's theory, it is quite possible that ᶜAli had it from Bachmann himself. How quickly a visitor's tale may develop into local tradition in these lonely villages, where nothing much happens and new stories or sayings are discussed and retold over and over again, we had proof of during the excavation of Jerwan, when things we had said during our visit the year before came back to us as "tradition."[11]

Bachmann visited Jerwan in 1914. After the war, when archeological research began again in Iraq, at least three scholars passed through Jerwan, namely Chiera, Speiser, and Thureau-Dangin. Speiser mentions his visit in a report to the American School of Oriental Research in Baghdad: "On our return we came upon a large dam near the village of Jerwana. Some of the inscribed blocks of the dam showed it to be the work of Sennacherib."[12] Of the visits of Chiera and Thureau-Dangin we were told by the villagers in the course of the excavation; and from subsequent correspondence with Thureau-Dangin we learned that during his visit he had discovered and copied the inscription referring to the bridge. On hearing, however, that we had succeeded in recovering the missing portions of that text he kindly agreed to refrain from publishing his copy.

[9] *Ibid.*

[10] See p. 2. The chief difference is that according to the story as told me the dam was built to keep back the waters of the stream so that the plain below would dry up. It is, however, quite possible that this is a misunderstanding on my part or on the part of my interpreter. The lake of which ᶜAli spoke may have been the reservoir behind the dam. This is supported by the fact that ᶜAli on a later occasion referred to the ruins as "a dam for irrigation purposes."

[11] A native told us that there was a story of how the king who built the bridge quarreled with his father and went away and built another city. We traced this back through several people, and the last man when asked whence he had the story answered: "From you, sahib. Don't you remember you told us this when you were here last year?"

[12] *Bulletin of the American Schools of Oriental Research,* No. 28 (1927) p. 16.

II

ARCHITECTURAL DESCRIPTION OF THE AQUEDUCT

The term "deep ravine" which Sennacherib applies to the depression spanned by the aqueduct at Jerwan does more than justice to what is in fact a mere wadi (Fig. 1; cf. front.). Of this, the bed of the stream which flows in it is naturally the deepest point. Its ancient level is marked by the platform of rough stonework which formed a foundation for the archways, and this is less than 7 meters beneath the pavement over which the canal water flowed. Thus, allowing about 2 meters for the parapet, the over-all height of the structure at the point where the arches occur would be about 9 meters. From this point, however, the sides of the wadi slope up gradually to the west and even more gradually to the east. As the width of the aqueduct without its buttresses is 22 meters and the total length more than 280 meters, it will be realized what a great mass of masonry is involved. If we assume the blocks of stone to average rather less than 50 centimeters cubed, the number of stones used would be well in excess of two million.

State of Preservation

The varying degrees of preservation of the various parts of the structure can in most cases be explained by studying the contours of the wadi (see Fig. 1). The extreme ends of the aqueduct, where it consisted merely of a few courses of paving flanked with parapets, would, together with the canal, first become choked and buried beneath the accumulating dust and débris; but the central portion, which stood higher above the ground, would remain exposed not only to the elements but to the depredations of those in search of stone ready cut for building purposes. It appears that the stream during its periodical floods was spending its force against the main bulk of stonework to the west of the arches; for here the greatest dilapidation has taken place, due no doubt to the continual undermining and erosive effects of the water. The ultimate destruction of the central portion may then have come about through blocks of stone swept down from this breach (Pl. VI*A*) obstructing the archways. The aqueduct would thus become a barrage across the wadi, and it would be only a matter of time before a volume of water would collect behind it sufficient to break through at the weakest point, namely where it was pierced by the archways (Pl. VI*B*). Then again, the pilfering of local builders would continue, facilitated now by the loosening of the blocks (Pl. VI*C*) and the breaking of the concrete pavement. In fact, we have ample evidence of the continuation of this pilfering process up to quite recent years, when a *mir* of the Yezidis made a substantial hole in the west half of the aqueduct by quarrying stone for a building project in ᶜAin Sifni.

The aqueduct as found by us, then, showed here and there the corner of a stone projecting above the turf—particularly on each side of the stream where it cuts through. Most of the south side east of the arches was overlapped by the village of Jerwan. At the east end of the latter a stone face bearing a telltale inscription disappeared beneath it. And the country for some distance around was conspicuously littered with fragments of limestone.

When our excavations were complete, the good preservation of some parts of the aqueduct proved a pleasant surprise (Fig. 2). At the east end a small section of parapet remained on the north (see Pl. IX*A*), also two courses of stone paving over a small area. The south face at this end had also been preserved, up to and including the concrete, almost as far west as

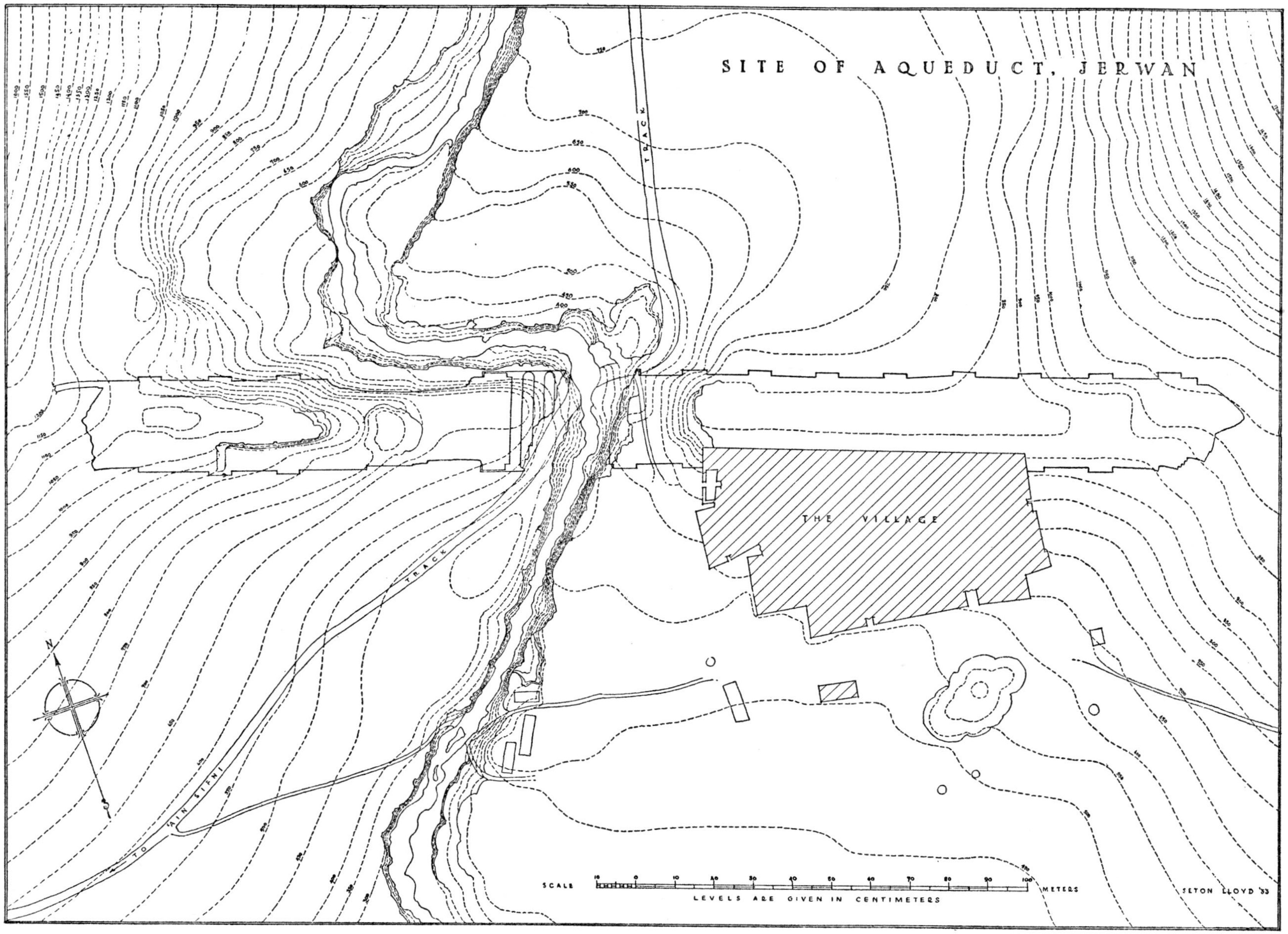

Fig. 1.—Contour map of Jerwan. Scale, 1:1500

the arches, by the modern village which is built against it (Pl. VII*A*). In fact, it seems reasonable to assume that at this point there was a contemporary settlement, perhaps of workmen employed on the aqueduct, and that the modern village is a survival of the ancient one. Another small area of paving was preserved a little farther along (Pl. VII*B*); we understand that this has just recently been greatly reduced by quarrying. North of this area the structure is scarcely more than denuded of the parapet. Copies of the standard inscription (*B*) are consequently preserved almost intact in five of the recessed bays and on four projecting buttresses.

At the west end of the aqueduct a large area of concrete is preserved, with small sections of stone pavement remaining in place at two points. But between here and the central arches considerable damage has been done by the stream to the north and by recent quarrying activities to the south.

A central breach cuts diagonally across the archways (Pl. VIII*A*), and since the bed of the stream has penetrated deeper the water has also carried away the major part of the foundation platform at this point. It was, however, extremely gratifying to find that sufficient remained of the westernmost two arch piers to permit almost complete reconstruction of this important section of the aqueduct (see Fig. 4).

The Foundations

It seems likely that the process of leveling in order to form foundations for the structure was begun at the deepest point of the wadi. Here a rectangular bed of rough bowlders was laid a little beneath the level of the stream, large enough to accommodate the six piers which were to support the arches. The bowlders were surmounted by a level pavement composed of big stones laid diagonally to the flow of the stream in order to increase their stability in time of flood; and from this rose the piers themselves (Pl. VIII*B*). A similar bed of rough bowlders was evidently prepared as foundation for the remainder of the structure, ascending the sides of the wadi to east and west in broad steps sunk in the side of the hill just deep enough to get a maximum support from the subsoil and at some points from the live rock beneath. This foundation was found in several places, projecting a little beyond the face of the buttresses, and it seems probable that it was originally laid to this width the entire length of the aqueduct.

The masonry was built solid from the foundation up to a point a little below the canal level, where a layer of concrete was spread. Upon the concrete was bedded an accurately graded stone pavement over which the water flowed. The height and coping treatment of the parapets which flanked it on each side are a matter of conjecture, since all that remains standing is a single course for some distance at one point in the northeast corner (Pl. IX*A*). Here, nevertheless, was sufficient evidence to establish the width of the parapets, together with various important points of stone jointing, the significance of which is discussed on page 15.

The Fabric

The façades are divided by projecting buttresses into fourteen bays, of which that containing the arches is twice the normal width (Fig. 2). The stones are for the most part cubic in shape and are laid in courses 50–60 centimeters deep. There are, however, two notable exceptions to this. First, large rectangular stones were used in the part adjoining the arches on each side and in the piers themselves. Naturally the stones which formed the actual corbeling of the arches were cut as long as possible for the sake of stability, and probably the increase in the size of the stones used for about 12 meters on each side of the central bay was for the same purpose. Second, in the facing of both buttresses and recesses the stones of alternate courses are a cube and a half in depth, so that the face is bonded properly with the structure

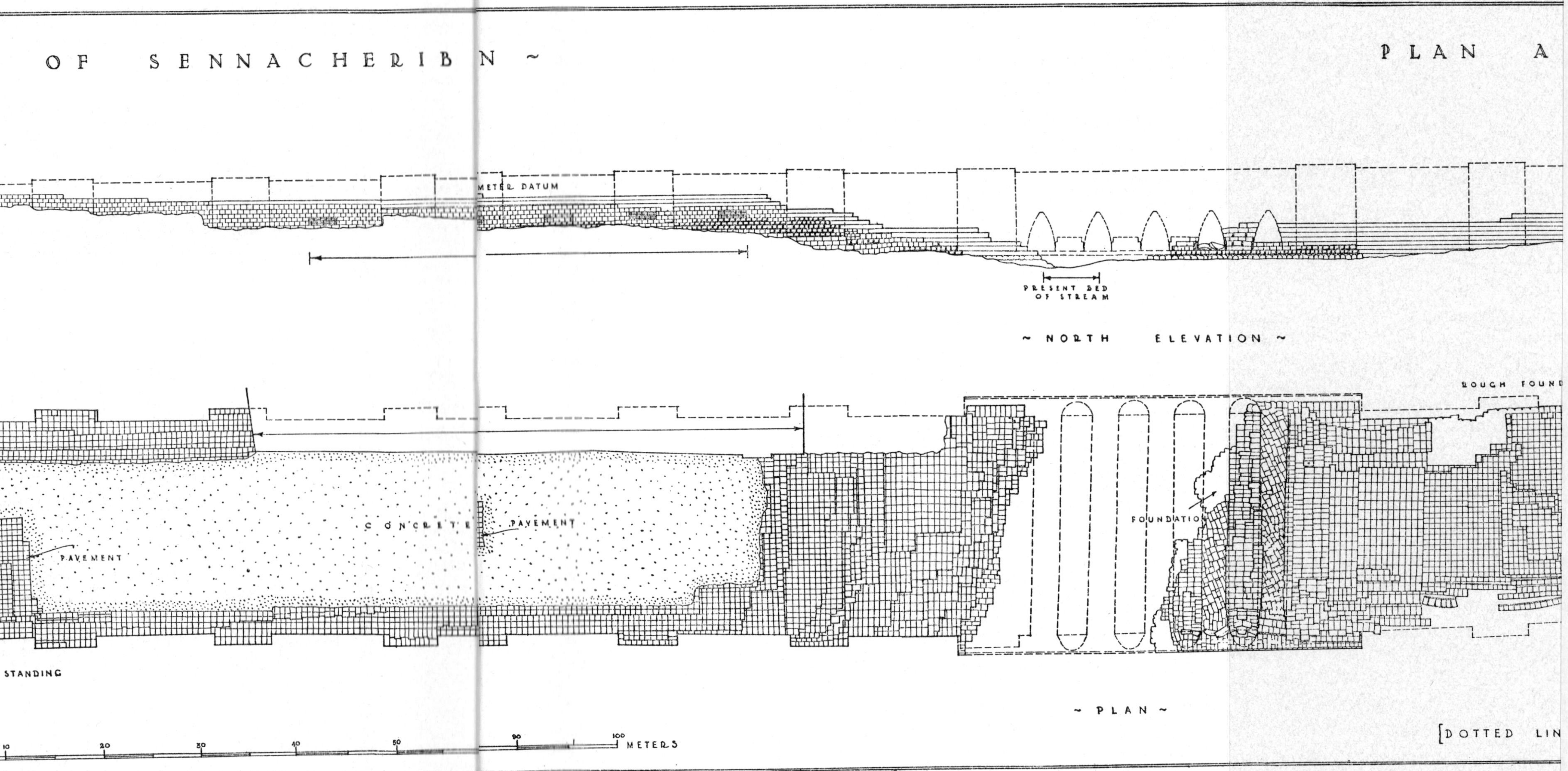

Fig. 2.—Plan and elevation of Jerwan aqueduct as existing. Scale, 1:500

irregularity in size of the blocks used and in the me
the fragments of inscription were not restricted to
(Pl. XI*A*). This irregular filling was seen to end an
exactly corresponding to where the inner face of th
had happened at this point became clear. At some
parapet had been breached by the pressure of the w
the outrush of water had carried away some of the
patched with stones discarded from some other buil
inscriptions appropriate to it. In repairing the dama
the filling as much as possible by widening it at the
pelled to retain the original line of the parapet. Th
both buttresses and recesses an extra projection in
been described, stepping back the masonry course b
old parapet.

THE STANDARD INS

The standard inscription (*B*), which we were able
of the north façade, is placed centrally on each but
third recess from the east end (see Fig. 2). It partia
which in some cases would be only a few centime
buttresses are more crowded than those on the rece
may be in proportion.

Mention is made on page 20 of certain fallen sto
fits neither of these proportions, and it is suggested t
along the parapet on one course of stonework only.

THE ARCHE

The remains of the westernmost two arches (Pl.
of the design of the central bay. A face equal at its
of a pier occurs between the first arch and the adjo
the façade and no doubt continued over the tops o
the tops of the projecting breakwaters. The arche
of being composed of radiating voussoirs placed in
device, but they were formed merely by corbeling out
it until ultimately the two sides met. The inner f
to any fairly flat curve but will necessarily produc
of the corbeling system. Our first arch remains stan
in reconstructing it to complete its extremely subtle
of the façade. A slight problem arises, however, in
the stonework at the apex. If we suppose that the
there are two methods of jointing. Either the poi
case a small vertical joint would appear on the face
joint, or it would coincide with a horizontal joint, w
curately the two featheredges of the uppermost sto
one of these treatments would be unsatisfactory fro
of view. In our reconstruction (Fig. 4) we have the
flat lintel stone to span the top of the arch a little

behind. A deep layer of stone chips at the foot of each façade bears witness to the fact that these facing-stones were worked by masons *in situ*. A similar impression is given by the fact that the mason in many cases adjusted the face of a stone to that of its neighbor only along the joint and left a rough projecting mass in the middle, thereby giving the appearance of intentional rustication (Pl. IX*B*). Over one large area to the northwest this technique seems more deliberate than elsewhere, for here the face of each stone is fairly well wrought, but all the edges have been cut back to a common lower level (Pl. IX*C*). This type of masonry has an extremely modern and sophisticated appearance and has not before been found in such early building. However, it is surprising to note how unsystematically these two types of rustication are scattered about the façades (cf. Pl. VI*B*). Often a solitary margined stone will appear in the middle of a large area of ashlar work. By analogy with modern designs, the heavier the rustication the lower it should appear in the elevation; but at one point a few stones of the parapet itself actually show this treatment.

The Repaired Breach

It will be well to mention here an irregularity which occurs at the west end of the south façade. Here in the first three bays the masonry is stepped downward, each course projecting a few centimeters beyond the one above it, until the lowest course is on a line with the normal

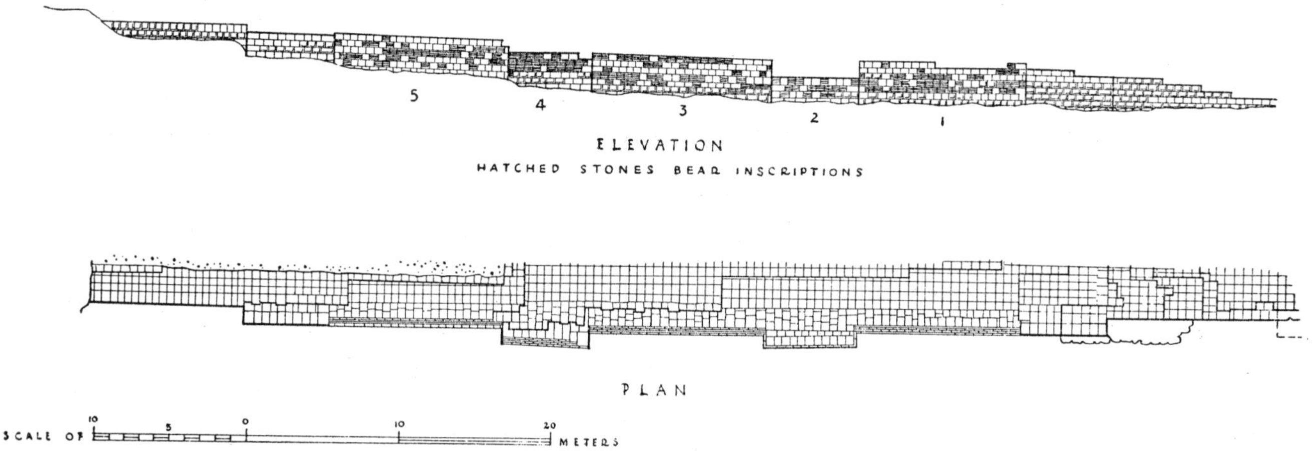

Fig. 3.—Details of the repaired breach. Scale 1:500. The numbers under the respective units of the wall correspond to those in Figure 7

face of the first and fourth buttresses; and the two buttresses separating these bays take their projection from this lowest face (Fig. 3). Thus a length of about 45 meters of stonework detaches itself from the rest of the façade, owing to its distinctive treatment; and the latter is accentuated by the fact that about half the stones used for facing in this portion bear fragments of a cuneiform inscription (see pp. 20 and 23–27) and appear to have been re-used here after being discarded from their original purpose and context. They occur haphazardly in the face of the masonry (Pl. X*A*), the signs sometimes reading from top to bottom and sometimes being partially obliterated, owing to the carving of a recessed margin such as has already been referred to.

It was not until the whole of this portion, including its upper surface, had been cleared that any explanation was forthcoming. A clearly defined section of the stonework behind this length of façade was then seen to differ from the surrounding fabric (Pl. X*B*) not only in the irregularity in size of the blocks used and in the method of laying them, but in the fact that the fragments of inscription were not restricted to facing-blocks but occurred farther in also (Pl. XI*A*). This irregular filling was seen to end and the normal masonry to begin at a point exactly corresponding to where the inner face of the parapet would occur, whereupon what had happened at this point became clear. At some time when the aqueduct was in use the parapet had been breached by the pressure of the water, or possibly by a hostile attack, and the outrush of water had carried away some of the stonework beneath. The breach had been patched with stones discarded from some other building, many of them still bearing traces of inscriptions appropriate to it. In repairing the damage the architect had wished to strengthen the filling as much as possible by widening it at the base, but at the same time he was compelled to retain the original line of the parapet. This was done by giving the base courses of both buttresses and recesses an extra projection in front of the normal face and then, as has been described, stepping back the masonry course by course until it was in alignment with the old parapet.

The Standard Inscription

The standard inscription (*B*), which we were able to uncover complete only on the east side of the north façade, is placed centrally on each buttress and in each recess beginning at the third recess from the east end (see Fig. 2). It partially covers two courses of stone at a height which in some cases would be only a few centimeters from the ground. The signs on the buttresses are more crowded than those on the recesses, so that the shapes of the inscriptions may be in proportion.

Mention is made on page 20 of certain fallen stones bearing traces of an inscription which fits neither of these proportions, and it is suggested that the standard inscription was repeated along the parapet on one course of stonework only.

The Arches

The remains of the westernmost two arches (Pl. XI*B*) provided very interesting evidence of the design of the central bay. A face equal at its base to rather less than half the breadth of a pier occurs between the first arch and the adjoining buttress. This is the normal face of the façade and no doubt continued over the tops of the arches as well as down the piers to the tops of the projecting breakwaters. The arches themselves are not arches in the sense of being composed of radiating voussoirs placed in position with some temporary centering device, but they were formed merely by corbeling out each course a little beyond the one beneath it until ultimately the two sides met. The inner faces of an arch thus formed may be cut to any fairly flat curve but will necessarily produce a pointed arch owing to the limitations of the corbeling system. Our first arch remains standing six courses high, and we are thus able in reconstructing it to complete its extremely subtle curve, used no doubt to enhance the design of the façade. A slight problem arises, however, in regard to the jointing and arrangement of the stonework at the apex. If we suppose that the two sides are actually brought to a point, there are two methods of jointing. Either the point would occur within a course, in which case a small vertical joint would appear on the face running from it up to the next horizontal joint, or it would coincide with a horizontal joint, which would involve bringing together accurately the two featheredges of the uppermost stones of the corbeling on each side. Either one of these treatments would be unsatisfactory from both a practical and an aesthetic point of view. In our reconstruction (Fig. 4) we have therefore preferred the alternative of using a flat lintel stone to span the top of the arch a little below the point at which the two curves would meet. The most notable precedent for this treatment is found in Minoan architecture and can be seen in the arches of the north viaduct leading to the palace at Knossos.

The lowest course of the inner face of the archway is 40 centimeters high and rusticated. The actual curve springs from the base of the second course; from here to the apex each course

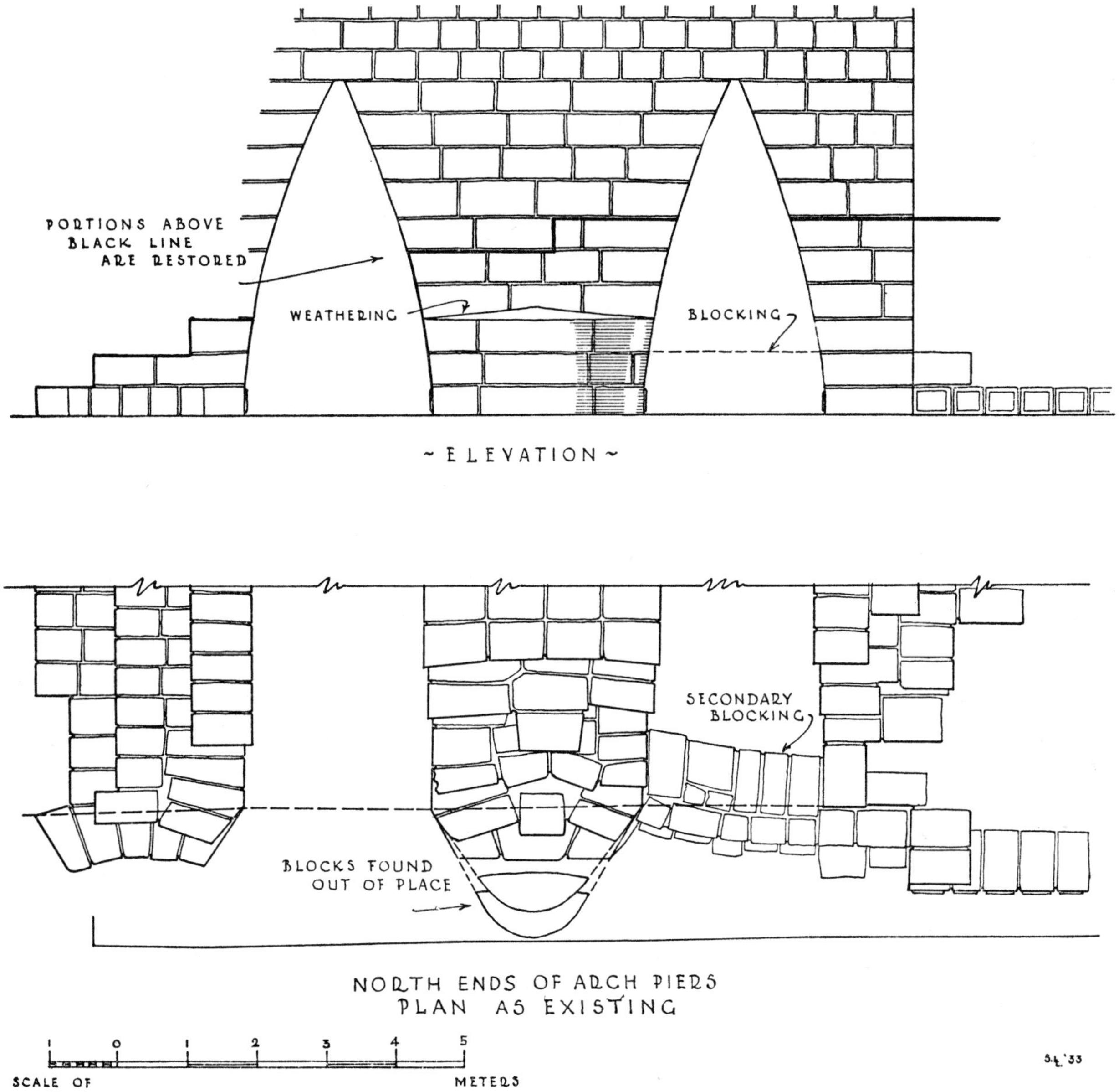

FIG. 4.—DETAILS OF THE ARCHWAYS. SCALE, 1:100

is precisely 50 centimeters. The face of each stone is not worked smooth, but the curve is gauged accurately from joint to joint (Pl. XII*A*). It has already been mentioned (p. 8) that the pavement upon which the piers were built and over which the stream flowed was composed of large stones laid diagonally to the axis of the archways.

The westernmost arch is partially blocked by a rough wall two courses high (see Pl. XI*B* and Fig. 4). It seems probable that both outer arches were treated in this way in order that the stream might normally utilize the three middle ones only, whereas the remaining two would come into play only on the occasion of a flood. It is also possible, however, that the blocking was the work of squatters who at a later date used this archway for shelter.

The Breakwaters

It has not been possible to reconstruct with absolute certainty the bastions or breakwaters which projected from the piers between the arches, owing to the extremely denuded condition in which we found their remains. But after carefully studying the curves of two stones which were wedged together in the mouth of the second archway (see Pl. XI*B*) in relation to the splayed sides of the bastion to which they obviously belonged, we see little possibility of an alternative to the treatment shown in Figure 4. The uninscribed semicircular stone would fit the splay angle of the lowest course, allowing room for a lost row of stones behind it, and would then terminate the projection a little inside the edge of the pavement. The next course is splayed at a slightly more acute angle; but the second, inscribed block, being differently shaped, would fit equally well here and allow the lower block to project slightly and form a kind of plinth. A third course identical with the second is indicated by the requirements of the inscription, but a fourth would have created an unsightly proportion and dwarfed the arches. Thus, with the addition of some sort of weathering on the flat top the bastion begins to take shape. It may possibly be objected that in our reconstruction the miter between the splayed sides of the projection and the curved face of the arch would involve a kind of double curvature which might test the ability of a mason. In the westernmost pier, however, sufficient remains of the second course to make the reconstruction certain. The splay on a single remaining stone (see Pl. VIII*B*) bears witness to the fact that such bastions were repeated as decorative features on the south ends of the piers, although their function as breakwaters would there be unnecessary.

The Crenelated Stones

The most puzzling find in the vicinity of the archways was a group of five stepped stones (Pl. XII*B*), in varying states of preservation, shaped as though each should form one unit of a line of stepped battlements such as are familiar in representations of Assyrian architecture. One was stepped on one side only, as though it belonged at the end of a row. Our first thought was that these might have crowned the main parapet, but a further consideration of their size and number put this completely out of the question. They are cut from blocks averaging about 55 centimeters high, 60 wide, and 30 thick. One need only draw a number of such blocks to scale along the top of the main parapet to realize at once that this could not have been their purpose. In fact, owing to their extreme smallness it has not been found practicable to suggest any position for them in our main reconstruction, although there are several possibilities. In more than one case the end which would be in contact with an adjoining block is splayed at a slight angle, which suggests that these blocks might have been used to decorate the tops of the projecting breakwaters. The positions in which they were all found, in the mouths of the surviving archways, might support this theory. Secondly, the wide expanse of stonework over the arches seems to call for some decoration or emphasis; and, if the splayed ends of these stones have no significance, their shallow depth would suggest that perhaps they formed ornaments in relief framed in recessed panels. A third possibility is that they occurred at some point in the masonry where special jointing was required.

The Pavement

One of the most interesting and significant points coming within the scope of this chapter is the great care and accuracy with which the stone pavement over which the canal water flowed was graded to an even fall (Fig. 5). It was clear that much more attention had been paid to the latter than would have been necessary had the passage of water alone been under consideration. This at once suggested the simplest solution of the problem as to how the stone was transported to the site. We had already proved to our own satisfaction whence it came by comparing fragments from the aqueduct with the limestone of the beds exposed in Sennacherib's quarry at Bavian. But at Bavian occurs also the head of our canal, which is connected with the Gomel River at a point where a great sculptured block (seen in the center of Pl. XIII) lies partly submerged in the stream. It seems probable that there occurred to the canal-builders the simple expedient of transporting their materials, particularly stone for aqueducts and other structures, over the level bed of the part of the canal which was already completed. If the blocks of stone were moved on wooden rollers or trucks, a fairly even surface would have been necessary, which is precisely what we find in the pavement of our aqueduct. If we imagine a carefully graded and paved way being available from the quarry to the site of the aqueduct, the transport of somewhat more than two million stones, each weighing about a quarter of a ton, seems a less formidable undertaking.

To return to the grading of the pavement in the aqueduct, it is fortunate that in the northeast corner sufficient remains of this part of the structure to give some idea of the ingenuity exercised by the builders in this respect. It has therefore seemed worth while to record our results in this section in detail.

The difficulty which we at once encountered in endeavoring to calculate the fall of the pavement was due to the uneven settlement which has taken place in the course of time. In some cases the irregularity was so great as to suggest some sort of seismic upheaval. In fact, the upper surface of the concrete at the west end is about half a meter higher than it is at the east; and, since the converse should really be the case, the possibility of comparing the levels at opposite ends is precluded. However, the fall between the two surviving sections of pavement at the east end of the aqueduct, measuring from the east edge of one to the east edge of the other, is at present about 80 centimeters in 64 meters (i.e., a fall of 1/80)—a ratio which accords with the kind of slope provided for in the system of jointing which we are about to discuss.

The stone pavement is laid on a bed of concrete about 40 centimeters deep—in other words, with the depth of an average stone course. It is evident that the concrete was intended partly to prevent the water from percolating through into the fabric of the stonework and, in the event of frost, splitting or disintegrating it. But the concrete does not extend beyond the inner face of the parapet on either side; and great pains were taken to prevent a straight joint between parapet and pavement. The precaution was obviously due to the fact that the constant weight of the parapet and the varying weight of the water might cause a crack and a consequent leakage of water. A tilting course (see Pl. IX*A*), such as has been found in some Babylonian paved streets, was used along the base of the parapet. This may have been designed for occasions when the aqueduct was not in use as such, to prevent water from collecting and standing at a vital point.

In Figure 5 we give a plan of the stonework as it exists at the juncture of pavement and parapet. It will be noted that a small section of pavement in the center of the figure and a

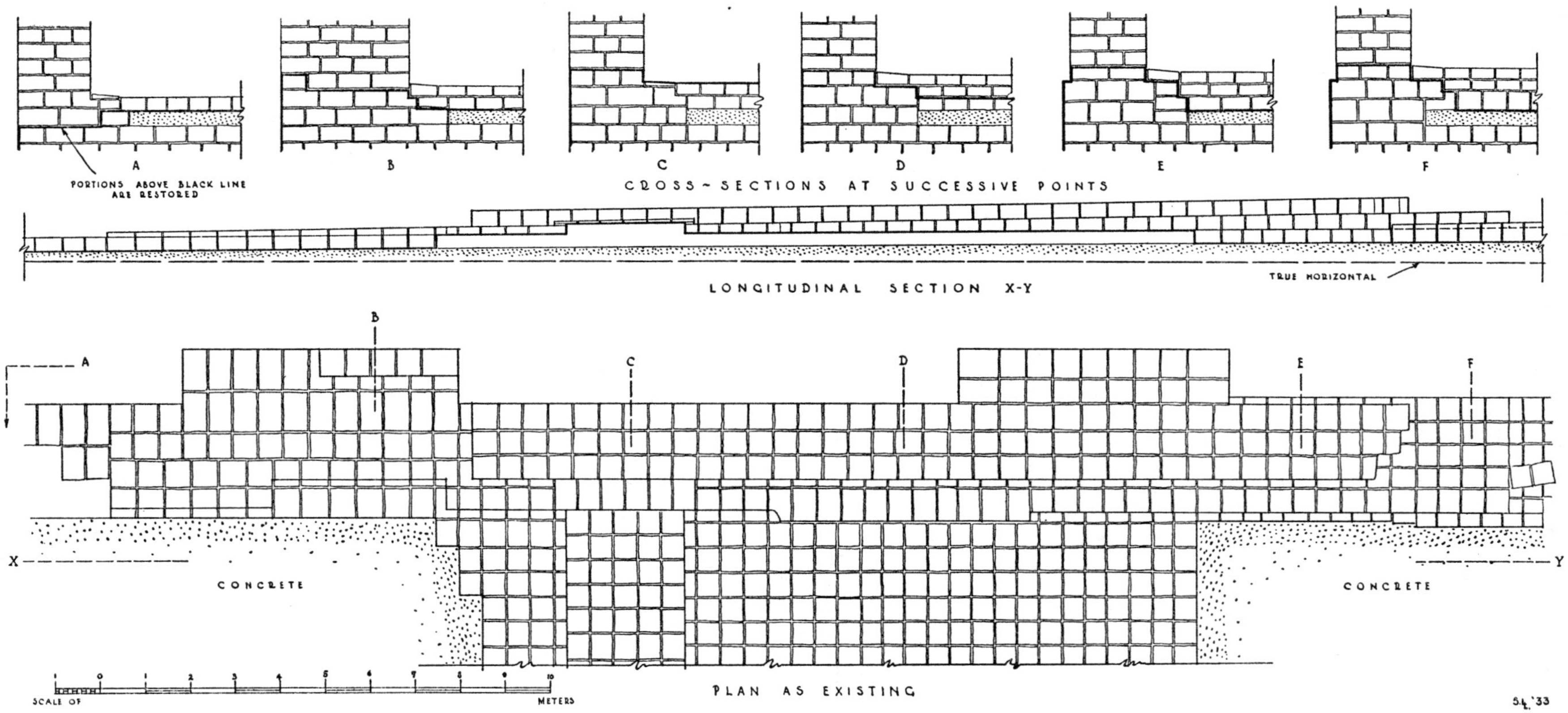

Fig. 5.—Drawings showing relation between parapet and pavement. Scale, 1:150

few stones of the tilting course (at *C*) are all that actually remains of the surface over which the water flowed. Above this in our figure is a longitudinal section looking toward the parapet, also as existing, while at the top are given successive reconstructed cross-sections, in each of which a thick line defines the part still existing.

The first indication we had of the accuracy with which the slope was graded was at the point marked *C* in Figure 5, where six stones of the tilting course remained intact (see Pl. IX*A*). These were all extremely thin stones, and they appeared to diminish in thickness from east to west at a rate which would bring them to a featheredge a few stones farther on. At precisely the point at which this would occur, however, the course on which they rest is stepped down, and the process of diminution was apparently begun afresh with a tilting stone about 20 centimeters deep sunk into the stone below. In order, however, to avoid a straight joint at the base of the parapet, this tilting stone continued beneath the latter, but here retained the normal depth of the course to which it belonged, with the result that at the point above referred to two curiously recessed stones occur which for some time proved extremely puzzling (see Pl. IX*A*).

At the extreme east end (*F* in Fig. 5) the stones on which the tilting course rested begin to be similarly recessed into the course below (Pl. XIV*A*). This also was difficult to explain, since everything above the latter had disappeared. However, after the grading of the pavement had been worked out, the only possible solution appeared to be that the pavement had consisted at this point of three courses of stones, which after some distance were reduced to two and then farther on to a single course. For it seems fairly certain, judging from the care with which the stones were wrought and laid, that the single course which survives in the center of the aqueduct about halfway between this point and the arches had carried the water on its upper face. It can only be supposed that from there onward the fall was maintained by making a step in the concrete and starting again on the lower level with three courses of pavement blocks. An argument in favor of this is the survival at the west end of the aqueduct of a section of pavement again consisting of two courses.

In the longitudinal section in Figure 5 it will at once be noticed that the upward slope of the concrete itself from the horizontal is too even to be attributed to settlement due to time. But the concrete seemed also to be of a uniform thickness. And the straight joint where it ends at the sides suggests that this also was contrived in order to assist in creating the correct slope on the pavement without interfering with the horizontality of the courses as they appear on the façade. The objection to this interpretation is that the horizontal joints as they now appear on the outer face of the structure everywhere show an incline. Accordingly it can only be presumed that this slope corresponded with that of the concrete, and that the piling of one paving course upon another was merely done to increase the fall.

The Concrete

Since the concrete (Pl. XIV*B*) played so important a part in the formation of a satisfactory channel for the water, we give here the results of an analysis made by the British Building Research Station in its Department of Scientific and Industrial Research:

> Samples of the concrete matrix, the limestone aggregate, and mortar from the stone joints were made available for examination, though only in small amounts. As a result of the examination it seems reasonable to assume that the concrete bed consisted of a mix made up of a magnesian limestone aggregate and muddy river sand, cemented by a magnesian lime made by burning a magnesian limestone.

EXAMINATION

The concrete matrix and the aggregate were both analyzed, with the following results:

		Concrete Matrix		Limestone Aggregate
Insoluble in acid	SiO_2	35.60	SiO_2	1.55
	Al_2O_3	18.30	Residue	0.80
	Fe_2O_3	2.10		....
	SiO_2	0.87		0.22
	Fe_2O_3	2.00		....
	Al_2O_3	7.34		....
	TiO_2	0.06		....
	CaO	13.90		33.30
	MgO	3.78		18.30
	CO_2	8.40		45.13
Loss on ignition (less CO_2, but including H_2O)		7.50		0.67
		99.85		99.97
	SO_3	trace		trace
	P_2O_5	trace		absent
	CaO:MgO	3.85:1.00		1.82:1.00

The matter from the matrix insoluble in hydrochloric acid was examined under the microscope and found to consist of a mixture of clay and fine sand. That is, it was a loamy sand.

CONCLUSIONS

The limestone is a pure magnesian limestone, quite high in magnesium carbonate though not a pure dolomite.

The concrete matrix is very friable and porous. Complete carbonation had not yet taken place. The matrix was apparently composed of a mixture of a sand and a burned magnesian lime. The present ratio between the two is 4 to 1 by weight, or about 2 to 1 by volume. If it were assumed that the lime used was obtained from the same source as the limestone used as aggregate and that the deficiency in the magnesia content of the matrix was due to the preferential leaching-out of the magnesia by water, since this amount of magnesia could not have been lost without some removal of lime it should be assumed also that the matrix was originally much richer, being composed of at least 1 part or more of magnesian lime to 1½ parts of sand [by volume]. The probability of such an assumption could best be judged from the variability of limestone deposits in the neighborhood and the constancy of their magnesia content. The sand contains a large amount of very fine material, and the sand grains themselves are not very rounded; it was probably a somewhat muddy river sand.

From the samples supplied it has not been possible to estimate the proportion of the large limestone aggregate to the matrix; but in a modern mix it would be expected that the ratio would be about 1½ to 1 by volume, which would give a general mixture of lime:sand:limestone of 1 :1½–2:4.

The Canal Parapets

At each end there is a fairly well defined point where the aqueduct proper ends and the canal begins. In both cases there are remains of the actual canal parapet disappearing beneath an unexcavated area of cultivated land. At the east end remains of the parapet occur on the north side only, the south side having subsided with the slope of the hill and been quarried away or removed. Here we uncovered one course of the canal parapet about 1.60 meters wide. This consists of stones somewhat bigger and less carefully worked than the majority of those used in the aqueduct and is composed of three rows of stretchers. The concrete or stone paving of the canal, if it ever existed, has been plowed up or destroyed from the point where the aqueduct ends. At the west end of the aqueduct occur remains of a stone pavement, consisting of two layers of small and somewhat carelessly laid stones, which projects considerably beyond the point where the aqueduct technically stops. This fact suggests that the whole length of the canal may have been similarly paved, but we have at present very little evidence for this.

Fig. 6.—Perspective restoration of Jerwan aqueduct

Here also we have remains of the canal parapet on the north side, standing three courses high (Pl. XV*A*),[1] again about 1.60 meters wide, and this time consisting of two rows of headers. The southward curve of this parapet indicates the way in which the canal began to swing round and follow the contour of the hill after crossing the aqueduct.

The Restoration

In suggesting a reconstruction of the façade (Fig. 6) only two points, namely the arches and the main parapet, require conjecture. The former point has already been discussed, and our solution of the latter we feel needs little defending. The use of projecting buttresses is the most common motive known in Assyrian architecture. By analogy with the palace and town walls of Khorsabad, where these are known to have projected a little above the normal parapet to form small towers, we have suggested a similar convention here, in order to break up the sky-line, as seen from below, in the most satisfactory manner from an aesthetic point of view. It is true that this would preclude the use of the parapet as a dry pathway when the water was flowing; but it could not have been more than a few hours' work to stay the flow of the water by means of the sluice gates mentioned in the Bavian inscription, so that men or chariots might pass dry shod along the canal bed and over the aqueduct.

[1] Only one course shows in Pl. XV*A*, but two foundation courses also were exposed on the side not seen.

III

THE AQUEDUCT INSCRIPTIONS

Inscription *A* (Pl. XVII)

Inscription *A*, the shortest of the inscriptions found on the aqueduct, would seem to correspond in form and purpose to the brick inscriptions of other Assyrian and Babylonian buildings; for it was found on a great number of the stone blocks incorporated in the fabric of the masonry. From the position of these stones within the fabric it was clear that the inscription was not intended to be read until the building had fallen into ruin (Pl. XV*B*). The text of this inscription reads:

šāt ^{md}*sin-aḫḫē*^{meš}*-rība*
šar$_4$ *kiššati šar*$_4$ ^{māt}*aššur*
Belonging to Sennacherib,
king of the world, king of Assyria.

The initial KUR of the inscription presents certain difficulties. It occurs again in an exactly identical inscription of Sennacherib on bricks found at Nineveh.[1] Elsewhere it interchanges with *ēkallu*, "palace."[2] The fact of this interchange led Delitzsch to suppose that KUR was an ideogram for *ēkallu;*[3] but in our case, in an inscription on an aqueduct, the meaning "palace" is obviously not to be considered. Another possibility would be to read KUR as *šadū*, "rock," which might do for the stone blocks of the aqueduct; but then it would be rather pointless in inscriptions on bricks. Other readings based on some ideographic value of KUR, such as *mātu*, "land," "country," or *kišittu*, "spoil," seem equally unsatisfactory. In the translation above therefore KUR is read phonetically as *šāt* and translated "belonging to," that is, as nominative feminine of *šū*. This reading seems to fit, as far as the meaning is concerned, in all the cases quoted, and it explains also why KUR in royal owners' labels may interchange with *ēkal*, "palace of." It might be objected that the form *šāt* would be an anachronism in an inscription of Sennacherib. This is true only in general, for we know that *šāt* survived in expressions such as *šāt mūši* and *šāt urri* down to Assyrian times. It would therefore not be surprising to find it again in a stereotyped formula for an owner's mark, as in inscription *A*.

Facsimiles of this inscription are given on Plate XVII. The fact that it is found reversed as well as normal suggests that the scribe cut it from above, lying flat on his belly on top of the stone upon which he was working. He realized that in cutting the inscription from above it was necessary to cut the heads of the vertical wedges near the top of the block; but he forgot to change the direction of the writing, and the result was not happy. That the scribe cut the inscription from above is probable only if we assume that the stone which he had to carve was already in position, and we may therefore deduce that all such stones were carved *in situ*.

Inscription *B* (Pls. XVII–XVIII)

Inscription *B*, the standard inscription of the aqueduct, was found in a great many places (Pls. XV*C* and XVI); but unlike inscription *A* it was always intended to be seen, and the signs accordingly are bigger and more carefully executed.

The places on the north side of the aqueduct where the standard inscription was found are indicated on the elevation in Figure 2. It occurs on every buttress and in every recess, except

[1] R. Campbell Thompson in *Archaeologia* LXXIX (1929) Pl. XLV 82 and p. 125.

[2] E.g. Rawlinson, *The Cuneiform Inscriptions of Western Asia* I (London, 1861) 48, No. 8:2; cf. *ibid.* No. 5:6 and No. 6:4.

[3] *Assyrisches Handwörterbuch* (Leipzig, 1896) p. 48.

west of the wadi where the masonry has become so dilapidated that no traces could survive and at the extreme east end where the aqueduct does not stand high enough from the ground to leave room for an inscription. Where the aqueduct crosses the stream we may suppose the standard inscription to have occurred on each breakwater, as it does upon the only surviving one (Pl. XVI*A*).

On the south side of the aqueduct it was found only once, namely on the buttress just east of the village. Beyond this the structure is not high enough for an inscription, but it is reasonable to suppose that it was repeated all along that section of the south façade now covered by the village. West of the wadi the south façade had been repaired (see p. 10) with stones bearing scattered fragments of inscription *D*, but it is possible that the original face of the aqueduct bore the standard inscription.

In all these copies of inscription *B* the text is arranged in nine lines. In uncovering the façades, however, we found a series of fallen inscribed blocks which, when pieced together, suggested that their text had been divided into only five lines of about double the usual length. At the points where these fallen blocks were found the standing masonry rose to a considerable height and bore the nine-line form of the inscription. The fallen inscribed blocks (Pl. XVII) must therefore originally have been situated at the very top of the aqueduct, perhaps in a band along the parapet. This would account for the difference in spacing.

The nine-line inscription found on the sixth bay from the west on the north side of the aqueduct is the best preserved copy which we found (Pl. XVI*C*). The lost portion, outlined in black in Plate XVIII, was restored from the inscription just east of it. All other copies of the standard inscription were collated, but no variations, either in orthography or in spacing, were found.[4] In transliteration and translation it reads:

^{md}*sin-aḫḫē*^{meš}*-rība šar*$_4$ *kiššati šar*$_4$ ^{māt}*aš-šur a-na šid-di*
ru-ú-qi mē^{meš} ^{nār}*ḫa-zu-ur ki-lal-la-an*
mē^{meš} ^{nār}*pul-pul-li-i̯a mē*^{meš} ^{āl}*ḫa-nu-sa*
mē^{meš} ^{āl}*gam-ma-ga-ra*
mē^{meš} *qup-pa-ni ša šadē*^{meš} *ša im-na ù šu-me-li*
ša i-ta-tu-uš-šú eli-šú uš-rad-di pat-tum
ú-šáḫ-ra-a a-na ta-mir-ti ninua^{ki} *eli na-aḫ-li*
ḫu-du-du-ti ša ^{aban}*pi-i-li pi-ṣi-i ú-šak-bi-is*
ti-tur-ru mē^{meš} *šá-tu-nu ú-še-ti-iq ṣi-ru-uš-šú*

Sennacherib, king of the world, king of Assyria, (says): "For a long distance, adding to it the waters of the twain Ḫazur River—(namely) the waters of the river Pulpullia—(and) the waters of the town of Ḫanusa, the waters of the town of Gammagara, (and) the waters of the springs of the mountains to the right and left at its sides, I caused a canal to be dug to the meadows of Nineveh. Over deep-cut ravines I spanned (*lit.*, caused to step) a bridge of white stone blocks. Those waters I caused to pass over upon it."

The somewhat unusual syntax of the first half of the inscription has necessitated a transposition in the translation. The clause *mē*^{meš} ^{nār}*ḫazur killallān . . . . eli-šúušraddī* was interpolated parenthetically in the sentence *ana šiddi rūqi pattum ušaḫrā*, indicating that the action recorded by the interpolation took place during the action recorded by the main part of the sentence.

The adjective *ḫududuti* (gen. pl. masc. of *ḫududu*) may be compared with Arabic خَدَّ, "fendre la terre, y faire des sillons"; خدّد, "être amaigrée, rider (la peau)." Another possibility would be to read *ḫu-ṭú-ṭú-ti* and derive it from *ḫaṭāṭu*, "to dig."

The phrase *ušakbis titurru* occurs also in cylinders of Sennacherib:[5] *i-na mi-iḫ-rat abulli qabal āli i-na a-gur-ri*

[4] An exception is the inscription on the breakwater, where the scribe wrote ^{nār}*pul-pul-li-i̯a* MEŠ ^{āl}*ḫa-nu-sa* instead of ^{nār}*pul-pul-li-i̯a mē*^{meš} ^{āl}*ḫa-nu-sa*.

[5] Published by B. T. A. Evetts in *Zeitschrift für Assyriologie* III (1888) 318, line 90.

abanpi-i-li pi-ṣi-i a-na me-ti-iq be-lu-ti-ịa ú-šak-bi-is ti-tur-ru, "opposite the gate of the inner city, for my royal passing, I spanned (*lit.*, caused to step) a bridge of baked bricks (and) white stone blocks." Compare also in another inscription of Sennacherib *i-na šuk-bu-us a-ram-me,*[6] "(storming a city) by bridging with planks (*lit.*, by causing planks to step [across the ditches])." The conception underlying this usage of *ušakbis* is that of the piers at each end as legs on which the bridge straddles the stream. The earlier translation of the phrase, "I caused a bridge to be walked upon,"[7] is less satisfactory, especially in the Jerwan passage, where the bridge in question was intended not to be walked upon but to carry water.

The standard inscription furnishes us with a considerable amount of new geographical information; for, although the rivers and villages mentioned do not appear in other texts, it is possible to locate most of them with a fair amount of certainty.

The name easiest to identify is that of the village Ḫanusa. This survives as Ḫines, the modern name of a small village near the Gomel River less than one kilometer south of the rock sculptures of Bavian. Bachmann states that Ḫines is situated on an artificial hill, a tell, from which he picked up a number of sherds. He further states: "Nicht weit westlich vom Plateau ist in der Seitenmulde zwischen der Anhöhe von Chinnis und dem Gebirge eine starke gute Quelle gelegen."[8] This spring, then, is clearly the "waters of Ḫanusa" mentioned in the inscription. Further proof of the identification may be found in the fact that we were able to follow the canal from Jerwan upward in the direction of Ḫines (see p. 30). The identification of Ḫanusa with Ḫines may therefore be considered as certain.

Since Ḫanusa is the only name in the inscription which seems to have survived as a modern place-name, in locating the other places we have to rely chiefly on the order in which they occur in the inscription. That this order is geographic, starting at the beginning of the canal and working down along its course, is suggested by analogy with the Bavian inscription, where the list of tributaries had been arranged in this manner (see p. 40). Further evidence may be found in the occurrence of a blank space after the last name of the list, Gammagara. The standard inscription was apparently destined not only for Jerwan but for all points of interest along the canal. The spacing and general arrangement of the inscription allowed for the inclusion of the names of all tributaries to the canal, but in carving the inscription at a given point the scribe would presumably insert only the names of such tributaries as had at that point already joined the canal and would leave blank spaces, such as that in the Jerwan list, for those which would join farther down the line. It is clear that such a process would result in a list of tributaries in the order in which they joined the canal.

Assuming, therefore, that the tributaries mentioned in the Jerwan inscription are enumerated in geographic order, we should look for the "waters of Gammagara," the last item in the list, between Ḫines and Jerwan; for the last tributary but one is the "waters of Ḫanusa," and Ḫanusa is modern Ḫines. In this section of the country, however, there is only one stream of importance, namely that which rises in the mountains above Shaikh Adi, passes Bingeli, and joins the Gomel midway between Ḫines and the Barrashah ford. This stream carries water all the year round and is consequently likely to have joined Sennacherib's canal. We may therefore identify it with the "waters of Gammagara" and locate that village at some point upon it.

Above Ḫines we should expect to find the rivers mentioned before Ḫanusa, namely the Ḫazur and the Pulpullia. In studying the map (Fig. 9) we are convinced beyond all doubt that one of those streams must be identified with the Gomel, which passes by Ḫines and is the

[6] Rawlinson, *The Cuneiform Inscriptions of Western Asia* I 39 iii 15.

[7] See Delitzsch, *Assyrisches Handwörterbuch*, p. 314: "betretbar machen, gangbar machen, pflastern"; Meissner and Rost, *Die Bauinschriften Sanheribs* (Leipzig, 1893) p. 17, note: "erbaute (liess ich betreten)."

[8] *Felsreliefs in Assyrien*, p. 2.

only big river which could supply the canal. But where is the other river? The passage concerned, *mē*^{meš} ^{nār}*ḫazur kilallān mē*^{meš} ^{nār}*pulpullia . . . . eli-šú ušraddī,* allows of two interpretations: (1) "Water from the twain Ḫazur River (and) water from the river Pulpullia . . . . I added unto it (the canal)"; (2) "Water from the twain Ḫazur River—(namely) water from the river Pulpullia—. . . . I added unto it (the canal)." If we choose the first of these translations we must account for two rivers north of Ḫines, namely the "twain Ḫazur" and the "river Pulpullia." Since each of these rivers has an individual name, both ought to be streams of some importance. For small streams were then as now named from some village which they passed and did not have names of their own. Now the Gomel is the only important river north of Ḫines; the upper Khazir is too far away to be considered, and the tributaries of the Gomel are merely small brooks which even at the present day are nameless. The first translation of the passage in question is therefore not probable.

The second interpretation assumes a single entity, the "twain Ḫazur River," which is defined more exactly as the "river Pulpullia." Since thus only one river is concerned, the expression "water from the twain Ḫazur" must refer to the Gomel. Now the Gomel is one of the two branches of the modern Khazir River, and the similarity between the names Ḫazur and Khazir is surely significant. If Sennacherib's Ḫazur actually represents the modern Khazir, his phrase "the twain Ḫazur" may refer to its two branches, the Gomel and the upper Khazir. To state that Sennacherib fed his canal from both branches of the Khazir would, however, not be in accordance with the topography of the region, for the canal was situated on the right bank of the Gomel and could therefore feed from this river only. For this reason, probably, Sennacherib modified his statement by adding "(namely) water from the river Pulpullia," which would thus seem to be a more precise definition to indicate that only the Gomel branch was concerned. Inserting modern equivalents for ^{nār}*ḫazur kilallān* and ^{nār}*pulpullia,* we might therefore translate: "Water from the twain Khazir—(namely) water from the Gomel branch— . . . . I added unto it (the canal)."

A few words should perhaps be said as to why Sennacherib used this somewhat circumstantial terminology instead of simply stating: "Water from the river Pulpullia (=Gomel) . . . . I added . . . . ." At the present day—and there is some evidence that similar conditions existed in Sennacherib's time[9]—the river with which we have been concerned above has as many as three names. The upper part of its course down to about Ḫines is called Atrush, from Ḫines to where it joins with the upper Khazir it is named Gomel Su,[10] and from there it forms part of the Khazir. Since "Khazir" is by far the best known of these names, it would not be unnatural to refer to the Gomel Su as "a branch of the Khazir, the Gomel Su." This is, in substance, not different from Sennacherib's phrase, and in a display inscription Sennacherib would be interested in using the most widely known designation possible.

Inscription *C* (Pl. XVIII)

Inscription *C*, which is merely an abbreviated version of the standard inscription, was cut in the upper surface of three blocks (one showing a break, so that they look like four in the facsimile) in the lowest course of a pier. The inscription must have been completely covered when the structure was intact and, like inscription *A*, must have been intended to be seen only after the aqueduct had fallen into ruins. The text reads:

[9] In the Bavian inscription, line 13 (cf. p. 36), Sennacherib says of the Atrush–Gomel Su: *kiribmāti-ịa panama nāru šuatu* ^{nār}. . . . *inambû,* "in my land they formerly called that stream . . . . ." This phrase suggests that on the border and outside of his country, i.e., in Urarṭu where the river rose, it had a different name, just as now the upper course is called Atrush, the lower course Gomel.

[10] "Su" is Turkish for "water," "river."

[1] [^{md}*sin-aḫḫē*^{meš}*-rība šar*$_4$ *kiššati šar*$_4$ $^{\textit{māt}}$*aš-šur*] *a-na šid-di ru-ú-qí ul-tu* $^{\textit{nār}}$*ḫa-zu-*[*ur pat*]*-tum ú-š*[*áḫ-ra-a a-na ta-mir-ti ninua*^{ki}] [2][*eli na-aḫ-li ḫu-du-du*]*-ti ša* $^{\textit{aban}}$*pi-i-li ú-šá-ak-bi-is ti-tur-ri mē*[^{meš} *šá-tu-nu ú-še-ti-iq ṣi-ru-uš-šú*]

[1] [Sennacherib, king of the world, king of Assyria, (says):] "For a long distance from the river Ḫazu[r] I caused [a ca]nal [to be dug to the meadows of Nineveh]. [2] [Over deep-cut ravines] I spanned (*lit.*, caused to step) a bridge of stone blocks; [those] water[s I caused to pass over upon it]."

The missing parts of the inscription have been restored from the standard inscription *B*. A comparison with that inscription shows that inscription *C* omits the list of tributaries, giving only the starting-point, the Ḫazur, and the end, Nineveh, of the canal. The section describing the bridge had of course to be retained, since the inscription occurred at this point in the canal; but, even so, it was shortened, leaving out *pi-ṣi-i* after $^{\textit{aban}}$*pi-i-li*. Orthographical variants are *ú-šá-ak-bi-is* for *ú-šak-bi-is* and *ti-tur-ri* for *ti-tur-ru*.

Inscription *D* (Pls. XIX–XXX)

Inscription *D* is unfortunately in an almost hopeless state of preservation. West of the wadi we found that the south façade of the aqueduct had been strengthened with a new shell of masonry (cf. pp. 9–10). A great many of the stones used for this purpose bore traces of an inscription; but it soon became clear that the stones, before they were used to strengthen the aqueduct, had formed part of some other building, on the façade of which the inscription had originally been carved. In re-using these stones no account had been taken of the old inscription, and fragments of it were consequently scattered haphazardly among uninscribed blocks (Figs. 3 and 7; cf. Pl. X*A*). In some cases the inscription had been turned sideways, in others upside down; but it seemed that generally the masons had placed the inscribed face outward, no doubt because it had the advantage of being already worked. The inscription had suffered serious damage when margins were cut on many of the blocks, so that not infrequently both the top and the bottom line of text have disappeared altogether. Since the remains of this inscription were found and cleared at a comparatively late stage of the excavation, it was possible to study only such inscribed stones as occurred on the face of the structure. There is reason to believe, however, that more inscribed blocks would be found if the masonry were taken down stone by stone.[11]

From the blocks which time permitted us to find it is possible to form a general idea of the arrangement and content of the original inscription. Some of the stones (Nos. 3, 34, 45, 92, 124, 129, 143, 191) have a vertical line near the left edge and must therefore have been situated along the left side of a column; whereas others (Nos. 61, 63, 128) have a vertical line at the right and must have been situated at the right side. For these vertical lines belong clearly to the frame of the inscription. The number of columns is suggested by Nos. 88, 136, and 170, where there are two vertical lines down the middle of the stone. These lines must represent frame lines of columns, and the stones on which they are found must therefore contain parts of two columns. The inscription thus had at least two columns. This assumption is supported by No. 124 also, which, according to the frame lines on it, must have come from the upper left-hand corner of a column. That column, however, cannot have been the first, for the signs in the first line read *a-na šu-*, which could not be the beginning of an inscription. No. 143 contains a lower left-hand corner.

Whether this inscription had more than two columns is more difficult to decide. Another valuable clue, however, is furnished by No. 124. Since this block from the uppermost inscribed course has only two lines of writing, and since the lines on all the known fragments of the

[11] Block No. 196 is actually from within the masonry (see Pl. XI*A*). It was situated to the left of block No. 2 in the row of blocks behind those shown in Fig. 7.

inscription run parallel with the long edges of the blocks, that is, with the courses of the masonry, the other inscribed blocks in that course can likewise have borne only two lines of

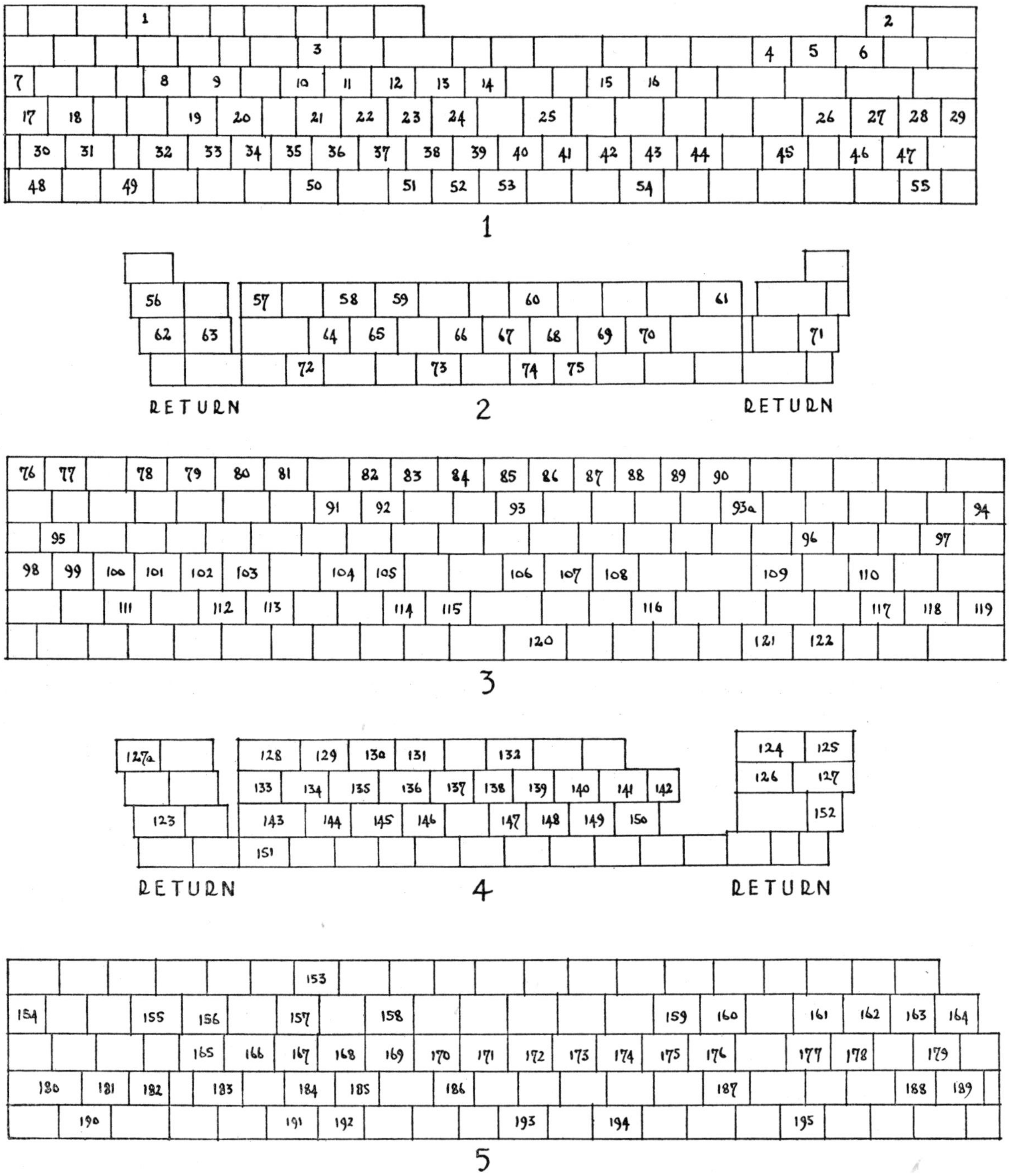

FIG. 7.—DIAGRAM SHOWING POSITIONS OF RE-USED BLOCKS INSCRIBED WITH PORTIONS OF JERWAN INSCRIPTION *D*

inscription. Now it is evident that the more columns the inscription had, the more such two-line blocks there must have been. In reality, however, such blocks are rare.[12] Hence in re-

[12] Besides No. 124 we found only Nos. 95, 97, and 120, and probably 93 and 161. Other possibly two-line blocks, too defaced or broken to permit certainty, are Nos. 1, 6, 12, 125–27, 127*a*, 155, 165–66, 169, 196, and 202.

constructing the inscription we should naturally restrict the number of columns to the minimum, which, as we have seen, is two. The corner blocks, Nos. 143 and 124, fit perfectly into this arrangement. The lower left-hand corner block No. 143 and its fellows in the same course (see p. 27) concern Merodachbaladan, who, though he figured in the fourth campaign, is most prominently involved in Sennacherib's first campaign. Hence this course may be assigned to the bottom of column 1. Its position there is confirmed by the words on the upper left-hand corner block No. 124. The latter evidently stands at the beginning of column 2, for it says: "To . . . . [. . . .] I entered [. . . .]," and these words occur in other texts dealing with the first campaign. The course containing Nos. 45 etc. (see p. 26) may be placed somewhere in the second column, since it mentions the city of Elenzi (elsewhere called Elenzash), which was involved in Sennacherib's second campaign.

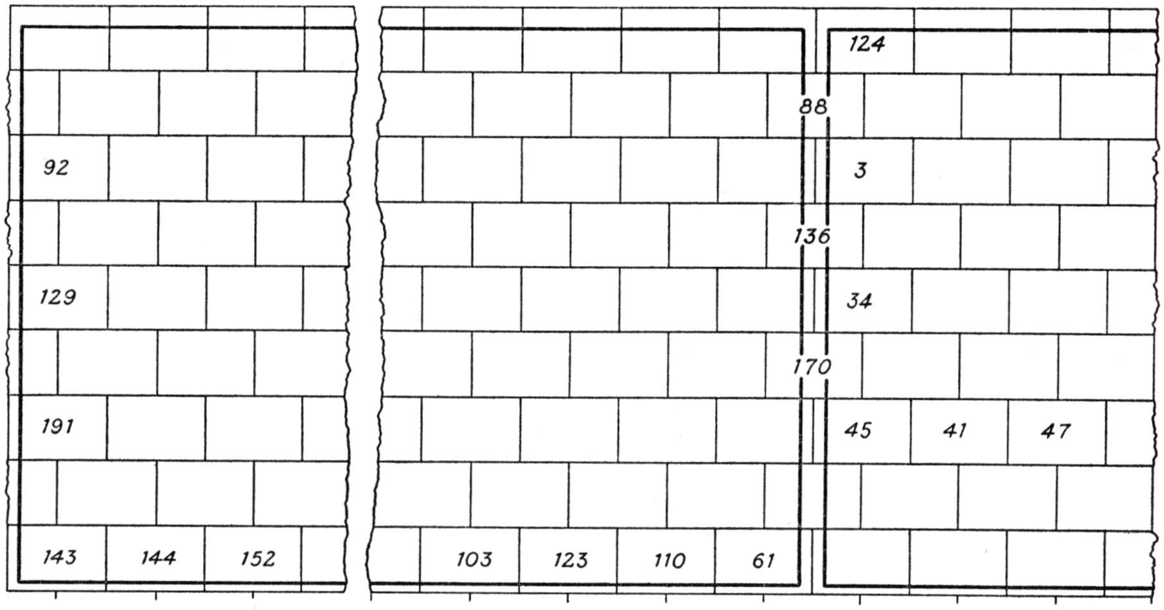

FIG. 8.—DIAGRAM SHOWING A POSSIBLE ORIGINAL ARRANGEMENT OF CERTAIN STONE BLOCKS BEARING PORTIONS OF JERWAN INSCRIPTION *D*

If there were only two columns and if the wall on which they were cut was bonded, then the three blocks with double vertical lines (Nos. 88, 136, 170), taken in connection with the eight with left-hand lines (including the corners Nos. 124 and 143), indicate a minimum height of nine inscribed courses (Fig. 8[13]), one with two lines, the others with three lines each. Thus there would be at least 26 lines in each column, making the inscription at least 52 lines long.[14]

The length of the lines is likewise uncertain; but, since in one case (p. 27) we can piece

[13] The most compact possible arrangement of the eleven blocks in question is represented. The 6 blocks with left-hand lines only have been divided equally between the 2 columns. Only No. 143 and its fellows and No. 124 are relatively fixed in position. Except for the fact that Nos. 45, 41, and 47 are definitely joined, the other numbers inserted are placed arbitrarily merely to account for the quantity and nature of the blocks involved in our reconstruction. The figure is schematic only; actually the double vertical lines on Nos. 88, 136, and 170 are not centered but lie toward the observer's right, and the margins on the eight blocks with left-hand lines are more than half as wide as the spaces found between the lines on the other three.

[14] The preceding paragraphs concerning the reconstruction of inscription *D* attained their present form only after a long and interesting discussion with Dr. T. George Allen, to whom numerous suggestions regarding the form as well as subject matter are due. The writer wishes to use this opportunity of expressing his indebtedness to the Oriental Institute's editorial staff as a whole for the care and interest which it has shown in dealing with this volume.

together three stones at the left of a column and four in the corresponding situation at the right and still have a considerable gap in the middle, each line must have occupied well over seven blocks. From traces of red color still adhering to some of the stones (Nos. 157, 165–66, 168, 171), it appears that the space occupied by the inscription was originally accentuated by a coat of red paint.

As indicated above, it seems likely that a number of inscribed stones still remain undiscovered inside the masonry. This impression is strengthened when we try to piece together the fragments we have, for it becomes evident at once that the material is far from complete. Furthermore, since no parallel to this inscription is known to the writer, the joins which we can offer are depressingly few. Even so, however, they suffice to give a rough idea of its original content. They are:

Nos. 26+20+29+27+60

. . . . *imēr*G]IR.NUN.NA*meš* *imēr*A[.AB.BA]*meš* *ù* [. . . .
. . . . *ú*]*-še-ṣa-am-ma šal-la-tiš am-nu* [. . . .
. . . . *ša n*]*i-ba la i-šu-ú ab-bul aq-qur* [. . . .

. . . . m]ules, camels, and [. . . .
. . . . I] brought out, as booty I counted [. . . .
. . . . with]out number I destroyed, I tore down [. . . .

Nos. 32+55

. . . . *āl*]*mar-ú-biš-ti* [. . . .
. . . .] *bīt šarrū-ti-*[*šu* . . . .
. . . . *al*]*-me ak-šu-du* [. . . .

. . . . the town of] Marubishti [. . . .
. . . . his] royal dwelling [. . . .
. . . . I sur]rounded, I captured [. . . .

Nos. 35+37

. . . .]*-ma kīma im-ba-r*[*i* . . . .
. . . .]*-ra-a šá ku-tal šād* [. . . .
. . . .] *šá li-me-ti* [. . . .

. . . .] and like a storm [. . . .
. . . .] . . . . which behind the mountain(?) [. . . .
. . . .] of the neighborhood [. . . .

Nos. 45+41+47

a-di a-na-ku a-na [. . . .
āle-li-en-zi [. . . .
aṣ-bat-ma šar(?) eš [. . . .

until I to [. . . .
the town of Elenzi[15] [. . . .
I seized and . . . . [. . . .

Nos. 69+121+67+117

. . . .]-MAŠ *amēla-su amēlda-gil-iṣṣūri* [. . . .
. . . .] *amēlnaggaru amēlkudimmu amēlnappaḫu amēl*[. . . .
. . . .] *ši-pir amēluš-par-ú-tu mu-du-ú* [. . . .

. . . .] . . . . , the physician, the auspex, [. . . .
. . . .] the carpenter, the silversmith, the smith, the [. . . .
. . . .] work of the weavers who know [. . . .

[15] Called Elenzash regularly in other inscriptions of Sennacherib.

Nos. 71+59

. . . .$^{\text{me]š}}$-*šú* ^{iṣ}*narkabāti*^{meš}-*šú* [. . . .
. . . .] *ú-nu-ut* É.[GAL-*šu* . . . .
. . . .] *i-na ki-rib* KÁ.[DINGIR.RA^{ki} . . . .

. . . .] his [. . . .]s, his chariots [. . . .
. . . .] the furniture of [his] pa[lace . . . .
. . . .] in the midst of Ba[bylon . . . .

Nos. 74+73

. . . .] *a-qar-tu ú-nu-u[t* . . . .
. . . .] ^{amēl}*man-za-az pa-ni* [. . . .
. . . .]. . . . *ú-še-ṣa-am-ma* [. . . .

. . . .] precious [. . . .], the furnitu[re . . . .
. . . .] the courtier(s) [. . . .
. . . .] I brought out [. . . .

Nos. 143+144+152+. . . . +103+123+110+61

i-na ūmi$^{[mi]}$*(?) im-ma(?)*-[. . . .] *abullāni*^{meš}-*šú*
a-na KÁ.DINGIR.RA^{ki} *ḫi-it-mu-[ṭiš* . . . .] ^{md}*marduk-apal-iddina*^{na}
šàr ^{māt}*kar-*^{d}*dun-ni-áš ša* [. . . .] *šu-a-tú ú-še-ṣa-am-ma šal-la-tiš am-nu*

in the day . . . . [. . . .] his gates
to Babylon speedi[ly . . . .]. Merodachbaladan
the king of Karduniash, who [. . . .]. This I brought out, I counted (it) as booty.

Nos. 164+109

. . . .]-KA *mul-mul* [. . . .
. . . .]-*na taḫāz ṣēri* [. . . .
. . . .]-*ma uš-še-ru ḫar-[ra-na* . . . .

. . . .] . . . . javelin [. . . .
. . . .] . . . . battle [. . . .
. . . .] and took the r[oad . . . .

The general phraseology of these fragments proves that the inscription originally recorded a series of campaigns. Names such as Marubishti and Merodachbaladan make it certain that the campaigns were those of Sennacherib.[16] Further than this, however, it is impossible to go; for our material is too incomplete to allow a more exact dating and it provides no clue to the whereabouts or nature of the building on which the inscription was originally carved.

[16] Cf. D. D. Luckenbill, *The Annals of Sennacherib* ("Oriental Institute Publications" II [Chicago, 1924]) esp. pp. 24 and 27–28.

IV

LEGENDS ABOUT THE AQUEDUCT

During our first visit to Jerwan the mukhtar, ᶜAli, had related a local tradition according to which the ruins behind the village were those of a dam (see p. 2). However, since this "tradition" resembles Bachmann's theory in all its essentials, in reality it may only reflect remarks made by him when he was surveying the ruins in 1914 (see pp. 4–5).

Sometime after our excavations had started, however, when we were settled in ᶜAin Sifni, we came across a new legend concerning the bridge. One evening when the physician, Dr. Petros de Baz, visited us, he mentioned a story which he had heard some weeks before from one of his patients as soon as the news had spread that we were coming to excavate at Jerwan. It ran as follows:

A king had a beautiful daughter whom two suitors wooed. The king declared that he would give his daughter to the one who first succeeded in supplying the village of Tell Kaif with water. On hearing this, one of the suitors set to work immediately on a great engineering project, to the magnitude of which the ruins at Jerwan still testify. The second suitor, on the contrary, was idle and sat all day in the coffeehouse until one day, when the work of the first suitor was well advanced, he went out and bought great quantities of white linen sheets. These he spread one beside another on the ground near Tell Kaif. Seen from afar they looked like water, and his plan succeeded. For when the first suitor saw the linen from far away, he believed that the other had already fulfilled the task; and his grief was so violent that he was taken ill immediately and died. The second suitor thus won the princess.

When the doctor told us this story we had been excavating for only three or four days, and no complete copy of the standard inscription had yet been found. We knew it therefore only in the fragmentary state quoted on page 2. That is, we knew that it mentioned a bridge and that Sennacherib caused something to pass over that bridge. This something we had imagined to be armies and war chariots. Now, on hearing the doctor's story, Lloyd suggested the possibility that, since the story clearly supposed the ruins to be part of a canal, our bridge might be an aqueduct and that which Sennacherib caused to pass over it might be water. Two days later this suggestion was put to the test. A well preserved copy of the inscription turned up on the north side of the bridge, and when we had removed the salt still obscuring the signs we read: "Those waters I caused to pass over upon it." The ruins, then, were those of an aqueduct. The doctor's story, thus surprisingly corroborated, took on a new significance.

In pressing our inquiries further, however, we were at first handicapped by the diffident attitude of the villagers, who seemed to consider such folklore somewhat childish and beneath their dignity. It therefore seemed best to approach them through the medium of our own workmen, whom we had brought from Tell Asmar and who were now quartered at Jerwan. Accordingly we instructed them to ascertain what they could on this subject.

The next morning it was raining when we arrived, and with all the men sitting around idle our opportunity for a chat seemed to be at hand. On inquiring of our Tell Asmar men what success they had had, we were told[1] that they had asked the old man in whose house they were staying about the story, and he had said that he had heard something like it once but had forgotten most of it. In the meantime ᶜAli (the mukhtar) and a few other villagers had come up, and I asked ᶜAli whether he knew any stories about the bridge. He answered that, as he had told me last year, it was said to be a dam. "But are there no other stories about it?"

[1] The ensuing conversation is taken from the daybook kept by the author during the excavation.

"No, sahib, no." "But I have heard a story about a king who promised his daughter to whoever could bring water to Tell Kaif. Is there not a story like that?" "Oh, well, yes, there is a story like that, but that is no good." "Never mind, tell it." Now ᶜAli is a cautious old man and will tell only what he himself finds credible. Even so, he generally adds: "This is what people say; but I do not know, perhaps it is only lies." In this case he evidently believed more in the story he had told us the year before; but he continued:

"Well, he put white cloth like this (he pointed to the white linen of a pair of trousers worn by one of the onlookers) on the ground near Tell Kaif." Here another man interrupts and proposes Tell Uskof; but he is overruled by the others, who stick to Tell Kaif. "Which city was he king of?" "He was king of Tell Kaif." "And the other one, where was he king?" "He was here (with a rather indecisive gesture embracing the region to the north and east); he wanted to bring the waters of the Gomel." "Of the Gomel? From where?" Now a man named Gharib takes up the story: "From Ḫines and then by the Gomel to Gerjinji." "Where is that?" "It is below Piyan." "And then?" "To Mamrashan and to here, to Jerwana." "And where does it go from here?" "To Baqasrah and to Baitnar." "And from there?" "To Maḥmudan perhaps." "And then?" "Then they don't say."

"But what were the names of these kings?" "We don't know." "Don't you know a single name?" "No, sahib (it is again the mukhtar speaking); you see we have nobody who can write and we have no books, so people tell from one to another and they forget." I try once more, but nobody knows. Then I remember Suliman Titi and ask: "But last year you told me about Suliman Titi. Wasn't he the king who built the bridge?" "No, no, he was not the king; he was only an *ustādh* (architect or engineer). The king we do not know." Then Gharib, who had spoken about the course of the canal, suddenly blurts out: "Nåshi-rawan, he was a king; he lived in Jeráhiyah." "Where is that?" "It is near Baᵓadrai where the *mir* lives, about half an hour's walk." "But has he anything to do with the story?" "Yes, of course he has; he was the father of the girl." This is the last bit of information to be had from them, and we drop the subject.

The story, however, was not limited to the village of Jerwan. We found that it was known also in the other villages of this region. Thus Khodaidah, the *agha* of Baqasrah, told us the whole tale much as Dr. de Baz had related it. In Khodaidah's version, however, the princess was in love with the second suitor; so when she saw that he was idle while his rival was well on his way to win, she sent for him and suggested to him the ruse with the linen. Khodaidah added also that the first suitor was buried on the north side of the bridge in a small mound which we had tried to excavate but had had to give up for lack of time. Regarding the course of the canal, he stated that it passed from Jerwan to Baqasrah, from there to Baitnar, then to Maḥmudan and via Kandalah to Shifshirin.

Further evidence of the ubiquitous nature of the story was obtained through the doctor, who informed us that the priest of the small Assyrian community in ᶜAin Sifni (see Pl. IV) knew it from his home in Baz, where it was current among the inhabitants. The Assyrians of Baz were known all over northern Iraq and in Armenia for their skill as masons and, according to the priest's version of the legend, had been instrumental in constructing the canal of the first suitor. Since Assyrians from Baz traveled considerably before the war and often visited the district around ᶜAin Sifni, they may have heard the story during such a visit and ascribed the work to their forefathers, who had been the skilled masons of this district for centuries.

The details concerning the course of the canal in the story suggested that definite traces of it must still exist. We therefore decided to spend a few days after the actual excavations were closed in searching for such traces. We succeeded in locating the canal in the following places (see Fig. 9):

Shifshirin.—At a point 1,500 meters east of the village we came across blocks of white limestone like that used at Jerwan. A tiny S-shaped wadi had cut across the ancient canal, exposing a cross-section (Pl. XXXI*A*). The stones thus exposed measured 80–90 centimeters by 60–70 centimeters. They were in position and indicated that the canal ran due east–west at this point. By measuring from one end of the stones to the other we found the width of the canal to have been about 19 meters.

Baqasrah.—Near here also stones like those at Shifshirin showed through the turf, and in places a terrace was cut into the hillside. Since the ground was cultivated, it was not possible to take exact measurements of the terrace, and so few stones showed above the surface that it would be necessary to dig in order to obtain any idea of the width of the canal here. From signs such as these we were able to follow its course almost to Jerwan.

Piran.—Beyond Jerwan we lost trace of the canal altogether until above Mamrashan in the fields southeast of Piran. Here we came across a terrace, similar to the one at Baqasrah, cut into the hillside. The terrace was perfectly level and obviously artificial. It measured 22 meters from side to side; and the measurements were easy to take, for the grass changed color very noticeably along a line on either side—a phenomenon due no doubt to a difference in the consistency of the ground.

We were unable to go farther, but were assured by local villagers that such a terrace can be seen at intervals continuing northward between this neighborhood (near the Gomel River) and Jiftah.

Bavian.—Our search ended at Bavian. We have nothing of importance to add to Bachmann's description of the sculptures and their surroundings. Our interest centered chiefly around a wide channel cut into the rock (Pl. XXXI*B*) some distance south of the sculptures. Bachmann speaks of it as a "langer Einschnitt am unteren Rand des Steilabfalls, der dicht am Fluss entlang läuft . . . . . Die durchschnittlich 7 m. breite Rinne ist in einer Länge von etwa 100 m. ganz deutlich zu verfolgen . . . . . Sie ist in den natürlichen Felsen eingearbeitet und endet im Norden an der gerade abschliessenden Felswand." Regarding the east side, Bachmann notes: "Hier münden zwei kleinere, kurze und gebogene Rinnen ein oder aus, deren Bestimmung unklar bleibt." Bachmann considers this channel "ein Baugraben für eine mächtige Stützmauer."[2] This explanation, however, is not very probable, for, as Bachmann himself had noticed, two smaller channels led from it to the river. The existence of these would be inexplicable if the large one were a "Baugraben." We noticed also that along the east side of the main channel there were low places in the natural rock which gave evidence of having been built up with masonry to a uniform height. It therefore seems more probable that this channel was some sort of watercourse—in fact, the beginning of our canal. Since we found it completely filled with earth, it was impossible to make any observations concerning its connection with the river or the possible existence of sluices; but further research might give interesting results.[3]

[2] *Felsreliefs in Assyrien*, p. 2.

[3] After these lines were written we had opportunity to investigate the points discussed here. Our new investigations confirmed our views expressed above. See chap. vi.

V

THE WATER SUPPLIES OF NINEVEH

As indicated by inscription *B*, the aqueduct at Jerwan and the canal to which it belongs (Fig. 9) were constructed for the purpose of supplying Nineveh with water. They thus take their places in that astounding succession of hydraulic engineering works by which Sennacherib transformed the barren environment of his new capital into a garden of almost paradisiac fertility. When Sennacherib, after his search for a place to which he might move the capital of Assyria, finally decided on Nineveh he must have realized how far this city fell short of his own ideal of a royal capital. The nature of this ideal is suggested in a passage where he blames "the kings my fathers" for the way in which they had neglected Nineveh: "Not one among them had given his thoughtful attention to,[1] nor had his heart considered, the palace therein, the palace of the royal abode, the site of which had become too small; (nor) had he turned his thought, nor brought his mind, to lay out the streets of the city, to widen the squares, to dig a canal, (and) to set out trees."[2]

The dream city of which we here read between the lines, with its spacious royal palace, its streets laid out according to a well considered plan, with broad public squares and all around it a belt of shady green gardens, is the royal capital which Sennacherib had in mind when he was planning the Nineveh of the future. And even in this brief summary of imaginary amenities it is easy to recognize some features reminiscent of Dūr Sharrukīn; for there also had appeared the sumptuous palace, the well planned net of streets, and the wide squares of which he speaks.[3] This we must attribute to the fact that Sennacherib had grown up in the very years when Dūr Sharrukīn was being built, years during which Sargon's conception of town-planning and the newest miracles wrought by his architects at Dūr Sharrukīn must have been the talk of the court. Maturing at such a time Sennacherib's ideal of a capital was bound to have much in common with that of his father, and special significance therefore attaches to the points in which his ideas diverge from this precedent and are characteristic of himself.

One such point is his insistence upon gardens and trees. Dūr Sharrukīn had no gardens around it. Square and unadorned its naked gray walls rose from the surrounding plain. But just as the uncompromising austerity which is so predominant in Sargon's character recedes in that of his son so as to form only the background for a richer and more versatile personality, thus also the hard mathematical rigidity of Sargon's capital is relieved in the city of Sennacherib by the mantle of green gardens growing around it.[4] It is this human trait in

[1] Expressed by *le-e-su ul id-da-a* (lit., "had not thrown down his cheek"). On *lētu*, "cheek," see P. Jensen in *Keilinschriftliche Bibliothek* VI, 2. Teil (1915) p. 5*. His explanation of the semasiological development through which "to throw the cheek" came to mean "to pay attention to" is less convincing. Probably "to drop the cheek," i.e., "to tilt the head sideways," had the same shade of meaning as our "to cock the head (inquiringly)." From this it is not far to "to give one's thoughtful attention to."

[2] Sidney Smith, *The First Campaign of Sennacherib* (London, 1921) lines 68 f., and Luckenbill, *The Annals of Sennacherib*, p. 95. The translations offered here and in the following pages are based on those of Luckenbill. Where my translations differ from his I have stated my reasons in the notes.

[3] Cf. Olmstead, *History of Assyria*, chap. xxiii, esp. pp. 271–72.

[4] It is of course not the intention to deny that a garden existed in Dūr Sharrukīn, for we have evidence for that; but that garden was confined to a corner of the palace platform and was not at all a prominent feature of the city. The gardens of Nineveh, on the contrary, grew all around the city and thus gave it its character.

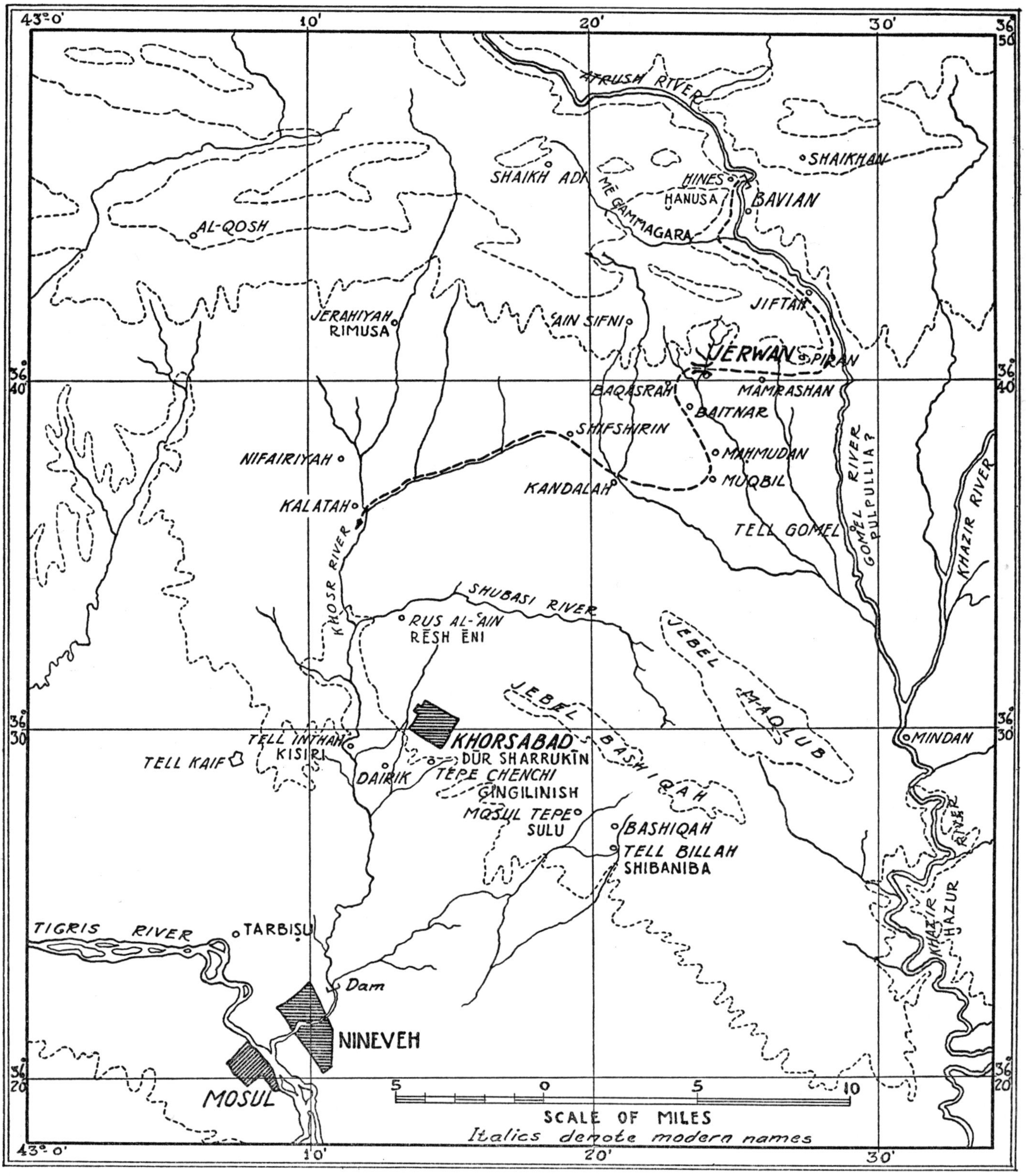

FIG. 9.—MAP OF THE REGION NORTH AND EAST OF NINEVEH, SHOWING APPROXIMATE COURSE OF SENNACHERIB'S BAVIAN-KHOSR CANAL

Sennacherib's character, his love of nature and his constant delight in parks and gardens, which is indirectly responsible for the magnificent system of water conduits which he created for Nineveh and which, spreading its tentacles farther and farther afield and drawing continually upon new sources, was ultimately to be responsible for the materialization of the capital of his dreams. Two years after Sennacherib's accession to the throne, in 703, he is able to speak of his first results:

A great park like unto Mt. Amanus, wherein were set out all kinds of herbs and orchard fruits,[5] trees such as grow on the mountains and in Chaldea, I planted by its (the palace's) side.[6] That (they might) plant orchards, I subdivided some land in the commons[7] above the city into plots of 2 PI each for the citizens of Nineveh and gave it to them. To make the orchards luxurious,[8] from the border of the town of Kisiri to the plain about Nineveh, through mountain and lowland, with iron pickaxes I cut and directed a canal. For a distance of [1½ *bēru*] I caused to flow there (i.e., in the canal) everlasting waters from the Khosr. Inside those orchards I made them run in irrigation ditches.[9]

The canal to which Sennacherib here refers drew its waters from the Khosr[10] and was, according to the inscription as restored, 1½ *bēru*, that is, about 10 miles,[11] long. This gives us a possibility of locating its starting-point, the town of Kisiri, which must have been situated 10 miles up the Khosr from Nineveh. Now a circle with Nineveh as its center and a radius of 10 miles would intersect the Khosr at the modern village of Qayin. A little south of Qayin, on the left bank of the Khosr, there is a small tell, Tell Inthah (see Fig. 9), which is the only tell in the immediate neighborhood and therefore would seem to be the site of Kisiri. That site being 10 miles farther up the Khosr, the level of the river bed was naturally considerably higher there than it was near Nineveh. By transferring the water from its natural bed to an artificial canal[12] which fell less steeply, it was possible, then, to retain a good deal of this height, so that

[5] Luckenbill transliterates *enibṣip-pa-a-te,* which he translates "fruit trees" (*op. cit.* p. 97, line 87). There is, however, no evidence that the sign GURU:*enbu* was ever used as a determinative. We must therefore consider the phrase as a *status constructus, enib ṣippāte,* "fruits of orchards," "orchard fruits," i.e., such fruits as generally grow in orchards.

[6] In the Kuyunjik Gallery of the British Museum this park is pictured on slab No. 55, which represents a scene from the construction of the palace at Nineveh. See British Museum, *A Guide to the Babylonian and Assyrian Antiquities,* 3d ed., pp. 55–56.

[7] Our rendering of *tamirtu.* This word, translated in many different ways, seems to derive from the same root as *amirtum,* which occurs in Old Babylonian letters. The latter, according to Thureau-Dangin (*Revue d'assyriologie* XXI [1924] 8, note 2), signifies "soit le fief, soit le territoire sur lequel on a authorité, dont on dispose comme administrateur." Our *tamirtu* accordingly might mean "commons," and the *tamirtu* of Nineveh would thus be the fields and arable lands held in common by the citizens of the city.

[8] Lit. translation of *a-na be-ra-a-ti šum-mu-ḫi.* For *berāti* as a synonym of *ṣippāte* and of *kirū,* "orchard," see Delitzsch, *Assyrisches Handwörterbuch,* p. 165. Originally *berāti* may mean "pits," as suggested by Delitzsch, and may designate the pits in which the trees were planted. The excavators found such pits in the garden of Sennacherib's *akītu*-house in Assur (*Mitteilungen der Deutschen Orient-Gesellschaft,* No. 33 [1907] pp. 24–32).

[9] S. Smith, *op. cit.* lines 87–90, and Luckenbill, *op. cit.* pp. 97 f. By some error Luckenbill's translation of line 90, *[1 1/2 bēru qaq]-qa-ru ul-tu ki-rib nārḫu-su-ur ma-a-me da-ru-ú-ti a-šar-šá ú-šar-da-a ki-rib ṣip-pa-a-te šá-ti-na ú-šaḫ-bi-ba pat-ti-iš,* has reference to the very similar lines in the version of the year 694 B.C. (*Cuneiform Texts from Babylonian Tablets, &c., in the British Museum* XXVI [1909] Pl. 33 viii 22 f.). The lost *1 1/2 bēru* has been restored from the Bellino cylinder (Layard, *Inscriptions in the Cuneiform Character* [London, 1851] p. 64, line 61). Apparently Sennacherib dammed the Khosr at this point and deflected some of its water into the canal which he had dug. Cf. the version of the year 694 (see above; translation modified from Luckenbill, *op. cit.* p. 114, lines 22–24): "The river Khosr, whose waters from of old took a low level and—(since) none among the kings my fathers had dammed them—poured (futilely) into the Tigris . . . . ." The *māme darūti* are "everlasting waters," not "flowing waters" as Meissner and Rost (*Die Bauinschriften Sanheribs,* p. 16) and Sidney Smith (*op. cit.* p. 77, line 90) translate; *ašar-ša,* "there," refers to the canal mentioned in line 89. On the various meanings of *ḫabābu* see my note 2 in *Acta Orientalia* VIII (1930) 69.

[10] The equation Ḫusur=modern Khosr was proposed by Pognon, *L'inscription de Bavian* (Paris, 1879) pp. 116–17.

[11] A *bēru* is 10,692 meters. See Thureau-Dangin in *Revue d'assyriologie* XVIII (1921) 133.

[12] The simplest way to do this would be by means of a weir (see p. 42). Now the town name Kisiri seems to derive from *kasāru,* "to dam (a river)," and may be the masculine form corresponding to *kisirtu,* "dam," "weir." It is therefore probable that Sennacherib utilized or renewed an old dam which already existed in this place and from which the town had its name.

it reached Nineveh at a level where it could be used for irrigation. And that was what Sennacherib did. The Kisiri canal placed as much water at Sennacherib's disposal as he could reasonably require, and he utilized it for watering the magnificent park which he had planted near his new palace. Since even then there was water to spare, he distributed plots of land above Nineveh so that the citizens might plant private orchards for their own pleasure.

These measures proved quite satisfactory for some years. The documents written in 702 and 700 B.C. repeat the first account without adding new features. Between 700 and 694, however, things began to move again. The original park beside the palace no longer satisfied Sennacherib, so he laid out new parks "above and below the city," where he planted "all the herbs of the land of Ḫatti (Syria), myrrh plants, among which fruitfulness was greater than in their (natural) habitat, all kinds of mountain vines"; in short, as he says: "All the fruits of (all) lands, herbs and fruit-bearing trees, I set out for my subjects."[13] In addition to irrigating these new parks, the original park, and the orchards of the citizens, the Kisiri canal was further used to water all the fields between Nineveh and the city of Tarbiṣu.[14] Thus its water-carrying capacity must have been taxed rather heavily.

How necessary it became to increase the water supplies of Nineveh we may gather from the fact that Sennacherib himself went out to investigate possible new sources. With great difficulty, so he tells us, he climbed Mt. Musri and succeeded in locating a number of springs and pools. The springs were enlarged, and the pools were turned into reservoirs from which a canal carried the water down into the Khosr. The additional volume of water obtained in this way was so considerable that it became possible to water his beloved orchards all the year round, even in summer when water grew scarce, while in winter the canal would carry water sufficient to irrigate as much as a thousand "fields" to the north and south of Nineveh.

It became evident, however, that in the spring, when the snow melts on the mountains and the smallest stream may develop overnight into a considerable river, the increased volume of water in the canal might become a menace. To avoid this it was necessary to arrange for some kind of an outlet, a safety valve which would break the power of the spring floods and regulate the flow. The way in which this problem was solved is most characteristic of Sennacherib. In the year 702 and again in 700 he had visited a country unlike anything else in his experience, when he pursued Merodachbaladan and Nergalushezib into the marshes of southern Babylonia. The beauty of that strange scenery must have taken hold of him; for now, confronted with the problem of an outlet for his canal, he solves it by making a marsh for himself, planting vast thickets of reeds and letting loose therein water birds, wild swine, and other creatures—the complete fauna of the Babylonian marshes. The account of these new undertakings is prefaced by an abbreviated version of the earlier works, the Kisiri canal and the gardens. Then Sennacherib continues:

To explore the waters[15] which are at the foot of Mt. Musri I took the road and climbed up and with great difficulty came to the city of Elmunakinne. At the head of the cities of Dūr Ishtar, Shibaniba, and Sulu I saw streams and enlarged their narrow sources and turned them into rivers(?).[16] To (give) these waters a course (through) the

[13] Luckenbill, *op. cit.* pp. 113–14, lines 16–21.

[14] Tarbiṣu is identical with Sherif Khan, a few miles northwest of Nineveh. Here Layard found bricks recording the building of a temple to "Nergal in the city of Tarbiṣu." See Layard, *Discoveries in the Ruins of Nineveh and Babylon* (London, 1853) pp. 598–99; British Museum, *A Guide to the Babylonian and Assyrian Antiquities*, 3d ed., pp. 36 and 73.

[15] Read *a-na bit-re-e ma-a-me . . . .*, with *bitrē*, "to explore" (infinitive I 2 of *barū*, "to see," "to investigate"), and *māme*, "waters," instead of the proper name "Bît-rêmâme" given by Luckenbill (*op. cit.* p. 114, line 31) and King (*Cuneiform Texts . . . . in the British Museum* XXVI, p. 29).

[16] The exact shades of difference between *namba*ᵓ, *ēnu*, and *kuppu* are not known. Each of these words seems to mean "spring," but according to our passage a *namba*ᵓ can be turned into a *kuppu* if the actual source (*ēnu*) is cleaned and enlarged. A *kuppu* would therefore seem to be larger and to have a greater output of water than a *namba*ᵓ.

steep mountains I cut through the difficult places with pickaxes and directed their outflow on to the plain of Nineveh. I strengthened their channels, heaping up (their banks) mountain high, and secured those waters within them.[17] As something extra[18] I added them to the Khosr's waters forever. I had all of the orchards watered in the hot (season). In winter a thousand fields of alluvium above and below the city I had them water every year. To arrest the flow of these waters I made a swamp and set out a canebrake within it. *Igirū*-birds,[19] wild swine (*lit.*, swine of the reeds), and stags[20] I turned loose therein. By the command of the god, within the orchards more than in their (native) habitat the vine, every fruit, *sirdu*-trees,[21] and herbs grew luxuriantly. The cypress and the mulberry, all kinds of trees, grew large and sent out[22] many shoots;[23] the canebrakes throve mightily. The birds of heaven, the *igirū*-birds, whose home is far away, built their nests; the wild swine and stags brought forth young in abundance. The mulberry and the cypress, the product of the orchards, (and) the reeds of the brakes which were in the swamp I cut down and used as desired, in the building of my royal palaces. The wool-bearing trees they sheared and wove (the wool) into garments.[24]

The theater of these operations is in general clear. Mt. Musri is known from Sargon's inscriptions to be modern Jebel Bashiqah, and recent excavation in Tell Billah near Bashiqah has established beyond doubt that this tell covers the ancient city of Shibaniba.[25] Elmunakinne, Dūr Ishtar, and Sulu, which are mentioned with Shibaniba, may therefore be looked for in the vicinity of Tell Billah. We know that, like Shibaniba, Dūr Ishtar and Sulu were situ-

[17] Luckenbill's translation of *mê*^{meš} *ša-tu-nu ki-rib-šú-un ú-kin-na* (*op. cit.* p. 115, line 40), "I brought those waters into them," does not quite do justice to *ukinna*. Sennacherib stresses that he confined the waters of the canals *securely* by means of the high embankments which he heaped up on either side.

[18] The reading *a-tar-tim-ma* and the translation "excess," "extra," suggested by P. Jensen (*Kosmologie der Babylonier* [Strassburg, 1890] p. 385) is preferable to *a-ḫaz-tim-ma*, "plan" (Luckenbill, *op. cit.* p. 115, line 41). See the discussion of this word in *Altorientalische Bibliothek* I (1926) 128, note 3, and the literature quoted there.

[19] KI.SAG.SAL^{mušen}:*igirū*. The Sumerian is probably to be read k i - e r u < *(i) k e r u, from which the Akkadians borrowed their word *igirū*. Cf. Howardy, *Clavis cuneorum* (Lipsiae etc., 1933) No. 81:134, and Deimel, *Šumerisches Lexikon* (Rom, 1925–33) No. 461:90. Our passage suggests that this bird was native to the Babylonian swamps and not found in Assyria; for from the Babylonian marshes Sennacherib got the idea for his swamp in Nineveh, and he states directly that the home of this bird was far away. Meissner in "Mitteilungen der Vorderasiatischen Gesellschaft" XV, Heft 5 (1910) p. 20, follows a suggestion from Delitzsch and translates "swan(?)," but as far as I know the swan does not occur in the Babylonian marshes. Another consideration speaks against the translation "swan." Most of what Sennacherib did had a utilitarian aspect. He states expressly that he used the reeds from the marsh in building his palace, that the cotton was used for garments, etc. Thus, since he took the trouble to import a bird, it is probable that he chose a game bird. The most impressive of the game birds found at the present day in the Babylonian marshes is the Goliath heron (see Bombay Natural History Society, *A Survey of the Fauna of Iraq, Made by Members of the Mesopotamia Expeditionary Force "D," 1915–1919* [Bombay, 1923] p. 333, No. 222), which thus seems to have a better claim to be Sennacherib's *igurū*-bird than has the swan.

[20] Luckenbill's reading *a-tan ki-ši*, "beasts of the forest" (*op. cit.* p. 115, line 58), is less convincing than Meissner's reading *a-lap(?) ki-ši* (*op. cit.* p. 20) and his tentative identification of this animal with the stags pictured on slab No. 56 in the Kuyunjik Gallery of the British Museum. If Meissner had realized that the slab with the stags is the very same as that which shows the swamp and the wild sow (see Layard, *Discoveries in the Ruins of Nineveh and Babylon*, pp. 108–9), he might have been more positive. For, since there can be no doubt that the slab actually pictures Sennacherib's marsh, it seems obvious that the stags pictured must correspond to the *alap kiši* of the inscription just as the wild sow corresponds to the "swine of the reeds" mentioned there; for these two are the only mammals to which it refers. Lastly, "ox of the forest" is not an unlikely designation for a stag.

[21] The ^{iṣ}*sirdu* is probably the bitter almond (Syr. ܫܓܕܐ). See R. Campbell Thompson, *The Assyrian Herbal* (London, 1924) pp. 131–32.

[22] From *ṣarāšu*, "to shoot branches." See Meissner and Rost, *op. cit.* p. 41, note 92. Cf. J. Hunger, *Becherwahrsagung bei den Babyloniern* ("Leipziger semitistische Studien" I, Heft 1 [1903]) p. 22, A 42 and B 9, where this verb is used of spurs on a star-shaped drop of oil.

[23] The word *papallum*, "shoot," is a synonym of *pirḫu*, "branch." See Delitzsch, *Assyrisches Handwörterbuch*, p. 533. The feminine of this word, *pappaltum*, seems originally to have had the meaning "bud," but is used chiefly as a euphemistic term for "glans."

[24] *Cuneiform Texts . . . . in the British Museum* XXVI, Pls. 34–36 viii 31–64; Luckenbill, *op. cit.* pp. 114–16.

[25] See *Bulletin of the American Schools of Oriental Research*, No. 49 (1933) pp. 14–15. The identification had already been proposed by Forrer, *Die Provinzeinteilung des assyrischen Reiches* (Leipzig, 1920) p. 35.

ated on mountain streams, and it is therefore probable that one of them is modern Bahzani, near Bashiqah on a mountain stream which carries water all the year round. The other may be hidden under Mosul Tepe, a tell on a small stream northwest of Bahzani. The name Mosul Tepe may even be a survival of the name Sulu. The canal which carried the waters of these streams down to the Khosr has not survived. From the map (Fig. 9), however, it seems likely that it followed the Bahzani stream down to Darawish. The wadi joining this stream on the left may represent the original Shibaniba branch. From Darawish the natural course is along the present Mosul-Bashiqah road to the point near Ortan Kharab where this road strikes a wadi leading down to the Khosr.

It is an interesting coincidence that, if Sennacherib's canal actually took the course suggested above on purely topographical grounds, it would have joined the Khosr at a small village now called Ajilah where R. Campbell Thompson found across the Khosr two dams which for quite different reasons he identifies as remnants of Sennacherib's marsh. These dams are situated one at each end of a defile through which flows the Khosr. The upper dam runs along the right bank of the river, then turns at right angles out into the stream. The lower dam, some 400 yards farther south, stretches diagonally across the river from the left bank; but it would seem that originally the river ran alongside the dam, and the place where it is now broken through may mark the position of an original sluice gate. Both dams are constructed of square stone blocks in Assyrian fashion. Behind the lower dam and originally protected by it lies a strip of low marshy ground where we may locate the swamp.[26]

The improvements to the canal system related above (pp. 34–35) were recorded in a document dating from the year 694 B.C. The next inscription which deals with the water supplies of Nineveh is the Bavian inscription written in 690. Although only the short span of four years separates the two, the picture which the Bavian inscription unfolds for us is on so vast a scale and so full of new features that it is scarcely recognizable. It reads as follows:

At that time I greatly enlarged the site (*lit.*, abode) of Nineveh. Its wall and the outer wall thereof, which had not existed before, I built anew and raised mountain high. Its fields, which through lack of water had fallen into neglect (*lit.*, ruin) and . . . . ,[27] while its people, ignorant of artificial irrigation, turned their eyes heavenward for showers of rain—(these fields) I watered; and from the villages of Masiti, Banbarina, Shapparishu, Kār Shamash-nāṣir, Kār Nūri, Rimusa, Ḫatā, Dalain, Rēsh Ēni, Sulu, Dūr [Ishtar], Shibaniba, Isparirra, Gingilinish, Nampa-gāte, Tillu, Alumṣusi, (and) the waters which were above the town of Ḫadabiti eighteen canals I dug (and) directed their course into the Khosr River. From the border of the town of Kisiri to the midst of Nineveh I dug a canal; those waters I caused to flow therein. Sennacherib's Channel I called its name.

The bulk of those waters[28] (, however,) I led out from the midst of Mt. Tas, a difficult mountain on the border of Armenia (Urarṭu).[29] In my land they formerly called that stream [. . . .].[30] Now I, at the command of Assur the great lord, my lord, added unto it (i.e., the canal) the waters of the mountains on its sides from the right and

[26] Thompson in *Archaeologia* LXXIX (1929) 114–15. Cf. R. Campbell Thompson and R. W. Hutchinson, *A Century of Exploration at Nineveh* (London, 1929) pp. 130–32.

[27] The words *ša-ta-a qé-e it-tu-ti* are difficult. Meissner and Rost leave them untranslated; Luckenbill (*op. cit.* p. 79, line 7) reads *ša-ta-a-ki-e it-tu-ti*, "came to look like pitch(?)." But *ša-ta-a-ki-e* would be a unique form, and the meaning "came to look like" seems purely conjectural. As a possible, though not altogether satisfactory, translation of these words and their context I suggest: "Its commons, which for want of water had become a wilderness and were covered (*lit.*, woven; 3d fem. pl. permansive I 1 of *šātu*, 'to weave') with spiders' webs (*lit.*, threads). . . . ."

[28] Luckenbill (*op. cit.* p. 79, line 12) translates *gu-pu-uš mē*^{meš} *šá-tu-nu* "the surplus of those waters"; but since the root *g p š* represents the idea of density, mass, bulk, probably the older translators were right in translating "the bulk of those waters." The author of the inscription must have been thinking of the waters of the canal as a whole, the bulk of which came from Mt. Tas, not of the waters from the 18 tributary canals which he had mentioned just before.

[29] TILLA^{ki} (Urarṭu, Armenia) might also be read URI^{ki} (Akkad). But already as early as 1879 Pognon (*L'inscription de Bavian*, p. 118) had realized that geographic considerations exclude the latter reading.

[30] The original name of this watercourse has disappeared. A restoration is suggested on p. 42.

left [and the waters] of Mê. . . . , Kukkut,[31] (and) Bīturra, towns in its neighborhood; with stones [I . . . .ed] the canal, (and) Sennacherib's [Channel] I called its name. In addition to the waters from springs and the waters which I had earlier secured by d[igging] (canals),[32] [. . . .] I directed their course to Nineveh, the great metropolis, my royal abode, whose site since [days of old the kings my fathers] had not enlarged and whose adornment they had not undertaken.

At this time I, Sennacherib, king of Assyria, first among all princes, who [marched safely][33] from the rising sun to the setting sun, [by means of] the waters from the canals which I had caused to be dug [. . . .ed] Nineveh together with its neighborhood; gardens, vineyards, all kinds of [. . . .], ... products of all the mountains, the fruits of all lands, and [. . . . I plan]ted. Up to (where) the waters could not reach I let them out over the thirsty ground,[34] so that its vegetation . . . . [. . . .] of all the orchards; on entering the lands(?) above (the city) and be[low(?)][35] from the midst of the town of Tarbiṣu to the "town of the Assyrian"[36] I irrigated annually (so that it was possible) to cultivate grain and sesame.

[Now] in intrusting that which I have planned to the kings my sons, [falsehood]s are not bef[itting].[37] W[ith] these few [. . . .] people[38] I dug that canal. By Assur, my great god, [I swear] that with these people I dug that

[31] According to Meissner and Rost, *op. cit.* p. 81, the reading ^{āl}*ku-uk-kut* is certain.

[32] In *eli mē*^{meš} *ku-up-pi ù mē*^{meš} *maḫ-ru-ti ša aḫ-*[*ru-ú*] (Luckenbill, *op. cit.* p. 80, line 16) the distinction drawn is one between natural tributaries of the Khosr (*mē kuppi*) and artificial canals or canalized rivers which Sennacherib had dug earlier.

[33] Luckenbill, *op. cit.* p. 80, line 19. Perhaps restore *šal-meš it-tal-lak-u-ma.* Cf. line 4 of the same inscription and Esarhaddon British Museum 12170 i 8.

[34] Luckenbill's translation of *a-di mē*^{meš} *la i-kaš-ša-du a-na ṣu-ma-me-ti ú-maš-šir-ma* (*op. cit.* p. 80, line 21), "setting free the waters where they did not reach the thirsty (field)," presupposes a text such as *a-šar mē*^{meš} *la i-kaš-ša-du.* But actually we have *a-di mē*^{meš} *la i-kaš-ša-du;* we must therefore translate: "Up to (where) the waters could not reach I let them out . . . . ." That is, "as far as the waters could go I let them out." The limit beyond which "the waters could not reach" is, of course, the contour line beyond which the ground level was higher than the level of the canal.

[35] Read *e-li-en āli(!) ù šap*[*lān*]. See Meissner and Rost, *op. cit.* p. 82, note 16.

[36] Read *a-di āli ša* ^{amēl}*aššur-a-a* (^{amēl}ŠÀ.URU-*a-a*), "up to the town of the ^{amēl}*aššuraʾa.*" This term means "citizen of the city of Assur." Cf. Koschaker, *Quellenkritische Untersuchungen zu den "altassyrischen Gesetzen"* ("Mitteilungen der Vorderasiatisch-aegyptischen Gesellschaft" XXVI, Heft 3 [1921]) pp. 75 ff. But it is out of the question that the area irrigated by the Khosr canal could ever have stretched as far as to the border of Assur, for the district of Kalḫu intervenes between Nineveh and Assur. On the borders of the latter see the first map in Forrer, *op. cit.* Luckenbill's translation (*op. cit.* p. 80, line 23) "to Nineveh" does not seem probable. It remains therefore as the only possibility to assume that "the town of the citizen of Assur" was some small town south of Nineveh, so named because it had been founded by a man from Assur, just as e.g. Kār Shamashnāṣir, "The Quay of Shamashnāṣir," was called after a man of that name.

[37] Owing to its bad state of preservation, the passage [*e-nin-na a-na*]*-ku* [*a*]*-na šarrāni*$^{\text{meš.ni}}$ *mārē*^{meš}*-ia ša it-ti lìb-bi uš-tam-mu-ma i-na qa-a-pi la tur-ru-*[. . . .]*-a-*[. . . .] is rather difficult. In endeavoring to restore and translate it we must start from two facts. First, *ša it-ti lìb-bi uš-tam-mu-ma* can mean only "that which I have planned (*lit.*, discussed with my heart)," for in this phrase *libbu* is always followed by a suffix which corresponds to the subject. In our passage *lìb-bi* must therefore represent *libbī*, "my heart." Second, *i-na qa-a-pi* must mean "in the act of intrusting," for such is the force of *ina*+infinitive. A translation such as "to believe" presupposes a text *a-na qa-a-pi.* We can thus translate the middle part of the passage, "in intrusting that which I have planned to the kings my sons." Sennacherib is therefore speaking of measures to be taken when his work is intrusted to later kings for repair and upkeep.

When the text again becomes clear we find Sennacherib taking a solemn oath verifying a statement as to the number of laborers and the time involved in constructing the canal. By giving this information in the form of a "sworn statement" Sennacherib emphasizes the fact that he is speaking the naked truth and not boasting. He evidently wants to show how comparatively inexpensive his work was in spite of its magnitude, so that a later king should not be afraid to undertake repairs or even restoration. It seems likely that Sennacherib might lead up to his oath by saying that under the circumstances only a strictly truthful statement would be of avail and then proceed to give his statement under oath by which he proved that he actually *was* speaking the truth. We may therefore restore the missing parts and read the entire passage [*e-nin-na a-na*]*-ku* [*a*]*-na šarrāni*$^{\text{meš.ni}}$ *mārē*^{meš}*-ia ša it-ti lìb-bi uš-tam-mu-ma i-na qa-a-pi la tur-ru-*[*ṣa ṣur-ra*]*-a-t*[*e*], "[Now] when I am in the act of intrusting what I have planned [t]o the kings my sons, [falsehood]s are not bef[itting]." I.e., a false boast would here be of no avail, for a later king would soon see for himself how much expense is involved. On *turruṣa* (3d pl. fem. permansive II 1 of *tarāṣu*), "are suitable," cf. the meaning "to be suitable" of *tarāṣu* I 1 (Bezold, *Babylonisch-assyrisches Glossar* [Heidelberg, 1926] p. 295).

[38] Restoration of *i-*[*na libbi*] is suggested by the following line, and Sennacherib's statement would make no impression at all on the reader if it did not indicate exactly how many men he employed. We can therefore be fairly certain that a number preceded ^{amēl}*ṣābē*^{meš}.

canal and in a year (and) three months I finished its construction, (and) [the day its construction(?)] had been completed I finished the digging of it.[39]

To open that canal I sent an *āshipu*-priest and a *kalū*-priest, and . . . . . Carnelian, lapis lazuli, *mushgarru*, *ḫulalū*, (and) UD.ASH-stones, precious stones, a BAL.GI-fish and a SUḪUR-fish, the likeness of [. . . .] of gold, herbs, (and) choice oil to Ea, lord of the springs, fountains, and meadows, (to) Enbilulu, lord of rivers, (and to) Eneimbal[40] I presented as gifts. I prayed to the great gods, and they heard my prayers and prospered the work of my hands. The sluice gate like(?) a [. . . .] or a flail was forced open inward(?) and let in the waters of abundance.[41] By the work of the engineer its (sluice) gate had not been opened when the gods caused the waters to dig [a hole] therein.[42]

After I had inspected the canal and had put it in order,[43] to the great gods who go at my side and who uphold my reign[44] sleek oxen and fat sheep I offered as pure sacrifices. Those men who had dug that canal I clothed with linen (and) brightly colored (woolen) garments. Golden rings, daggers of gold, I put upon them . . . . .[45]

At the mouth of the canal which I had dug through the midst of Mt. Tas I fashioned six great steles with the images of the great gods my lords upon them, and my royal image in the attitude of salutation[46] I set up before

[39] Read *ni-iš* ^{d}*aš-šur ili-ia rabī* [*at-ta-ma-a*] *šum-ma ina libbi* ^{amēl}*ṣābē*^{meš} *an-nu-ti nāru šu-a-tu la ú-šaḫ-ru-u ù i-na šatti* (MU.AN.NA) *3 arḫi la ú-qat-tu-ú ši-pir-šá la* (cf. Meissner and Rost, *op. cit.* p. 76, line 26) [*ūm ši-pir-šá(?)*] *ig-gam-ru-ú ú-qat-tu-ú ḫi-ru-sa.* Luckenbill and the earlier translators overlooked the fact that we have here the construction with *šumma . . . . la* as used in oaths, and that accordingly the clauses with *la* should be translated as positive.

[40] Luckenbill (*op. cit.* p. 81, line 29) reads ^{d}*bēlē*^{e} *nappalti-*[*ia*] and translates as "the lords who answer my prayers(?)"; but, since we do not know what *nappaltu* actually means, it seems safer to read ^{d}*en-e-im-bal* and assume with Meissner and Rost (*op. cit.* p. 76) that it is the name of a deity. Probably the name means "the lord who digs canals" (^{d}e n e i - n - b a l (- a)>^{d}e n - e - i - m - b a l (- a)), which might well be the name of some minor Sumerian deity.

[41] Luckenbill (*op. cit.* p. 81, lines 30–31) translates *bāb nāri* [. . . .] *ù* ^{iṣ}*narpasu a-na ra-ma-ni-šu ip-pi-ti-ma ú-šar-da-a mē*^{meš} *nuḫši* "a canal-gate (sluice-gate) [I built] and the sluice-valve opened by itself and supplied the water of abundance." Meissner and Rost leave the doubtful part blank in their translation (*op. cit.* p. 77), but in their notes (*op. cit.* p. 84) they translate ^{iṣ}*narpasu* as "Dreschschlitten" and believe that it represents a sluice gate because both sluice gate and threshing sledge would be heavily studded with nails.

These translations, however, are not quite satisfactory. In the first place, *ana ramani-šu* occurs in no other passage with the meaning "by itself," which is regularly represented by *ina ramani-šu.* The meaning of *ana ramani-šu* is "for itself," "to itself"; cf. e.g. *ana ramani-ia aṣbat,* "I took for myself," and see the passages quoted by Delitzsch, *Assyrisches Handwörterbuch,* p. 624. The sluice gate thus opened "to itself," "toward itself," which perhaps means "inward."

In the second place, the translation of ^{iṣ}*narpasu* as "threshing sledge," which is the basis for Meissner and Rost's and Luckenbill's identification of it with a sluice gate or valve, is anything but certain. Its translation "threshing sledge" is derived from its ideogram ^{giš}MAR.ŠE.RA.AḪ (=^{giš}MAR.ŠE.RAḪ), "a sledge (^{giš}m a r) (for) threshing (r a ḫ) grain (š e)." Bur ^{giš}m a r is the source of Assyrian *marru* and still exists in the Arabic of Iraq as *marr,* "hoe." So we might just as well translate "a hoe(-shaped object for) threshing grain," which would change the ^{iṣ}*narpasu* from a threshing sledge into a flail. That the latter translation is, in fact, the better one may be seen from other ideograms for *narpasu.* Thus ^{giš}MAR.TAG means "a ^{giš}m a r (for) beating." This description fits only the flail, with which the grain is beaten, not the threshing sledge, which is pulled across the grain. Another ideogram for *narpasu,* ^{giš}AL.TAG, corroborates this idea, for it means "an *allu* (for) beating," and *allu* is a kind of hoe. See Thureau-Dangin in *Revue d'assyriologie* XXI (1924) 145. Finally, the very derivation of *narpasu* (<**ma-rpas-um*) should be mentioned, for *narpasu* <**ma-rpas-um* must mean "tool for beating." The ^{iṣ}*narpasu* seems therefore to be some sort of flail.

The damaged signs 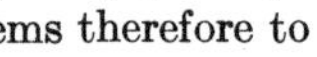 might perhaps be restored as  . We might then read the whole as *bāb nāri* ⌜*ki*⌝-[*ma*] *qa*[*l*$_4$-*p*]*i ù* ^{iṣ}*narpasu a-na ra-ma-ni-šu ip-pi-ti-ma ú-šar-da-a mē*^{meš} *nuḫši,* "the sluice gate was opened (i.e., forced) inward, (looking) like an adz or a flail, so that it allowed to flow the waters of abundance." I.e., the waters rushing through a hole which they had dug forced the lower part of the sluice gate inward and upward, so that it looked like the blade of an adz or the swingle of a flail.

[42] Read with Meissner and Rost (*op. cit.* p. 76, line 31) *i-na ši-pir qatē*^{II} ^{amēl}*itinnu* (^{amēl}DIM) *la ip-pi-*[*ti*], "by the work of the engineer's hands it was not opened." Luckenbill's reading (*op. cit.* p. 81) with *amēlûtimtim,* "through man's handiwork," is not convincing. Restoring the lacuna in the passage which follows, we may read [*i-nu*]*-ma* [*pil-šu i-na*] *lìb-bi ilāni*^{meš} *ú-šáḫ-ru ma-a-me,* "when the gods caused the waters to dig [a hole] therein." Luckenbill's restoration and translation, "for the heart's comfort(?) of the gods I dug water(courses)," does not account for the plural form of *ušaḫrū,* which indicates that *ilāni*^{meš} is the subject.

[43] Luckenbill's translation of *iš-tu nāru ap-pal-su-ma uš-te-eš-še-ra ši-pir-ša* is: "After I had planned the canal and directed its construction."

[44] Read *mu-kin-nu palē-ia(?)* with Meissner and Rost, rather than *mu-kin-nu bal-tu(du),* "who establish prosperity," with Luckenbill.

[45] We omit the account of the Babylonian war (Luckenbill, *op. cit.* pp. 82–84, lines 34–54).

[46] On the rocks the king is pictured raising his hand toward his face (Bachmann, *Felsreliefs in Assyrien,* Pls. 9–11). That therefore must be the *lābin appi* gesture mentioned in the inscription (Luckenbill, *op. cit.* p. 84, lines 55–56). The

them. Every deed of my hands which I had wrought for the good of Nineveh I had engraved thereon. To the kings my sons I left it for the future[47]. . . . .

From among the numerous details presented by the Bavian inscription we can disentangle four large undertakings: (1) the excavation of eighteen canals, which all joined the Khosr; (2) the canalization of the lower part of the Khosr itself, from Kisiri to Nineveh; (3) the irrigation of Nineveh, the planting of parks and orchards, etc.; (4) the construction of a new canal from Mt. Tas. Since this last canal is the principal subject of the Bavian inscription, we learn numerous details concerning it, such as the names of its tributaries, its renaming, the time required for its construction, the nature of the opening ceremonies, and the description of six sculptures which the king set up at its outlet.

Some of the undertakings here commemorated are known from Sennacherib's earlier inscriptions. The second project, for example, deals with the Kisiri canal, the king's first attempt to supply Nineveh with water. The third project, the irrigation of the environs of Nineveh, may easily be identified with the previous enterprise on the same lines, though the area affected by the canal has by now grown to include the whole left bank of the Tigris from Tarbiṣu down to the "town of the Assyrian." In the first project three of the eighteen canals mentioned are recognizable, namely those of Sulu, Dūr Ishtar, and Shibaniba, which constituted the Mt. Musri system of 694 B.C.

After the undertakings referred to in the earlier inscriptions are eliminated there remain sixteen canals, including the one from Mt. Tas, to which the scribe pays particular attention, which presumably did not exist four years earlier. All contributed to the Khosr. In trying to locate these sixteen new canals it seems advisable to start with the first project, in the very center of which the older canals of the Mt. Musri system are mentioned. The fact that the Musri complex occurs here in the group suggests that the list was drawn up in geographic order, for otherwise we should expect to find the Musri complex mentioned at the beginning and the new names simply added to the older ones. This impression is strengthened in the cases where we are able to identify the towns named in the inscription with modern localities. Such cases are—besides Sulu, Dūr Ishtar, and Shibaniba which we have mentioned above—the cities of Rimusa, Rēsh Ēni, and Gingilinish.

Rimusa is known from other texts to have been the seat of an Assyrian prefect. It must therefore have been a fairly large city. Now there are in the region with which we are dealing only two tells large enough to suggest anything but an ordinary village, namely Tell Gomel and Jerahiyah. Of these, Tell Gomel is out of the question, for it is situated in the plain of Navkur on the left bank of the Gomel River at a point from which a canal could not possibly have been directed into the Khosr. Jerahiyah, on the other hand, not only meets our requirements for size but lies on a tributary of the Khosr, just as Rimusa should do according to the inscription. It therefore seems fairly certain that Jerahiyah is Rimusa.

There is nothing to suggest that Rēsh Ēni and Gingilinish were more than small Assyrian villages. But the names themselves come to our aid, for they seem to survive in the modern place-names Rus al-ᶜAin and Tepe Chenchi.

Rus al-ᶜAin, meaning "fountainhead" as does Rēsh Ēni, is marked on older maps near the outlet of the Shubasi River, apparently in the vicinity of Raqabah Hamdan. Since Rēsh Ēni

---

Sumerian equivalents for *lābin appi*, k a š u - g á l (or more correctly k a - a š u - g á l) and k a š u - t a g, confirm this, for they mean "to place (g á l) the hand (š u) upon the nose (k a - a)" and "to tap (t a g) on the nose (k a - (a)) with the hand (š u)." The verb *labānu* in *lābin appi* must therefore have some such meaning as "to stroke," which is not far from the meaning "to mold (bricks)," also attested for *labānu*. In any case, the old translations of *labān appi*, "*proskynēsis*" or "die Nase platt machen," should be abandoned.

[47] Read with Meissner and Rost (*op. cit.* p. 78, line 57) *a-na šarrāni*$^{\text{meš}.ni}$ *mārē*^{meš}*-ịa e-zib(!) ṣa(!)-ti-iš*. Luckenbill (*op. cit.* p. 84) read the last words as *e-piš-ti-iš* and translated "to be a memorial(?)."

should have been situated on a tributary of the Khosr and since the Shubasi River is such a tributary, the similarity of the names Rus al-^{c}Ain and Rēsh Ēni may justify their identification.

Finally, we may connect Gingilinish with the little hill called Tepe Chenchi,[48] situated south of Khorsabad on a small stream. This stream, which carries water all the year round, flows into the Khosr, and in the name Chenchi (*čenči*) < Kenki we have the first and essential part of the name Gingi-l-inish. An investigation of the hill by the Iraq Expedition of the Oriental Institute in the spring of 1933 furnished evidence that it had been inhabited in the Assyrian period. This evidence, together with the similarity of name and situation, fairly establishes the identity of the two places.

If we now compare the locations of the villages which we have identified with their positions in the list we find that in traveling down the Khosr we seem to pass Jerahiyah, Rus al-^{c}Ain, Jebel Bashiqah, and Tepe Chenchi in exactly the same order as the corresponding names Rimusa, Rēsh Ēni, the Mt. Musri group (Sulu, Dūr Ishtar, and Shibaniba), and Gingilinish appear in Sennacherib's enumeration.[49] We may therefore accept the order of names in the list as geographic, a fact which will assist us considerably in locating approximately the other villages mentioned in the inscriptions.

According to this principle we should expect to find the villages Masiti, Banbarina, Shapparishu, Kār Shamashnāṣir, and Kār Nūri, which precede Rimusa in the list, farther upstream than Jerahiyah, the modern equivalent of that town. Here, however, the objection must be met that Jerahiyah itself is situated almost at the source of the Khosr. The Khosr rises in the mountains near Balatah. On its way down into the plain it passes Jerahiyah and is joined a little above Nifairiyah by two small streams coming from ^{c}Ain Baqrah and from the region of Baiban. Farther down, at Kalatah, it is met by another stream, which comes from Shifshirin. Now at Kalatah it is difficult to decide which is the main river and which the tributary, for both carry about the same amount of water. Thus, although the western branch, coming from Balatah, Jerahiyah, and Nifairiyah, is nowadays considered to be the actual Khosr, it is possible that in Sennacherib's time the Shifshirin branch was considered the more important of the two and should be identified with the Khosr of his inscriptions.

This assumption is supported by two important facts. First, we know that the main body of Sennacherib's canal, which followed the Khosr below Kalatah, followed the Shifshirin branch above this city. Secondly, the inscription includes the canal of Rimusa among the tributaries of the Khosr. Now we have already identified Rimusa with Jerahiyah, so that the tributary of the Khosr which in Sennacherib's time flowed past Rimusa must be the stream nowadays called the upper Khosr. Since, however, Sennacherib refers to it as a tributary, his Khosr must have been elsewhere; that is, it must have been the Shifshirin branch. If we grant that the Shifshirin branch was Sennacherib's Khosr, the difficulty in connection with Masiti, Banbarina, Shapparishu, Kār Shamashnāṣir, and Kār Nūri disappears immediately. These sites may be looked for along the numerous minor tributaries which join the Shifshirin stream from the north.

The villages mentioned after Rimusa—Ḫatā and Dalain—are probably between Kalatah and Rus al-^{c}Ain (Rēsh Ēni) on the Shubasi River, perhaps in the actual valley of the latter. The list continues with Sulu, Dūr Ishtar, and Shibaniba, which are to be found in the Jebel

[48] This mound was called "Tepe Shenshi" in Frankfort, *Iraq Excavations of the Oriental Institute, 1932/33* ("Oriental Institute Communications," No. 17 [Chicago, 1934]) p. 89. A later investigation among the inhabitants of the village named from the tell showed, however, that "Tepe Chenchi" is the correct form. Also on the official map No. $\frac{\text{J–38}}{\text{T}}$ (1:253,-440) the name is written with *ch*, "Chanchi."

[49] On the map Tepe Chenchi comes before the Jebel Bashiqah group. That it is mentioned after the latter is due probably to the misleading impression received on the ground by one traveling down the Khosr.

Bashiqah, and ends with Isparirra, Gingilinish, Nampagāte, Tillu, Alumṣusi, and Ḫadabiti. Of these we have already identified Gingilinish with Tepe Chenchi. Isparirra, which precedes it, may well be modern Tell Dairik, which is situated a little northwest of Tepe Chenchi on another small watercourse. The rest remain problematical; we can only deduce that they might be found in the plain between Jebel Bashiqah and Nineveh.

Having located as far as possible the towns from which the eighteen canals were named, we have yet to deal with that mentioned last in the Bavian inscription, the Mt. Tas canal which forms the main subject of that text. In addition to the topography of the canal, upon which subject the inscription is so full of information, we have the story of its construction and learn of a curious incident in connection with it.

When in 690 B.C. the work drew near its completion, having lasted for a year and three months, Sennacherib sent out two priests to perform the rites necessary to insure the success of the work. At the same time he presented precious gifts to the two gods, Ea and Enbilulu, who were specially concerned with springs and rivers. In spite of these precautions, however, a mishap occurred. Before the engineers in charge of the work were ready to open the sluices, the pressure became too great and a breach occurred, presumably behind them.

An unexpected occurrence of this sort suggests to us only a miscalculation on the part of the engineers; but to the ancient Assyrians it took on a more sinister aspect, for it might have been interpreted as an ill omen portending the displeasure of some god at this interference with his river. Sennacherib, however, found a better explanation of the portent. Actually no serious damage had been done. The waters, it is true, had broken through without waiting for the engineers to open the sluices; but the final result was nevertheless very much the same. Clearly, therefore, the gods were not angry. On the contrary, overanxious to see the canal completed, they had "caused the waters to dig."

Accordingly, having satisfied himself with this happy explanation, Sennacherib traveled to where the mishap had occurred, inspected the damage, and, having put things in working order, offered new sacrifices to the gods. The engineers and workmen, who must have lived in trepidation during the time which elapsed between the mishap and the king's visit, were pleasantly surprised to receive splendid garments, gold rings, and gold daggers instead of losing their heads, as they might well have done had the interpretation of the omen been otherwise.

Besides this and other details of the history of the undertaking, the inscription contains much information on the topography of the canal. Of primary importance is the statement that Sennacherib erected at the "mouth" of the canal steles bearing representations of the principal gods; for these steles can be no other than the rock sculptures at Bavian, where the inscription was carved. Since Bavian is thus shown to lie near the "mouth" of the canal, the canal itself is evidently the Gomel River, which flows out immediately below the sculptures. That Sennacherib's canal proves to be a natural river need not astonish us, for the term used by him, *nāru*, actually means "river." This particular canal was in fact a canalized river and not an artificial watercourse. This is made clear by the inscription itself, where we read that the stream had an earlier name before Sennacherib started work on it and renamed it. It must therefore have existed as a watercourse before that time.

The statement that the sculptures at Bavian were placed at the "mouth" of the canal shows furthermore that the main body of it should be sought north of this point. That is, it must represent the modern Atrush River, as that part of the Gomel which is above Bavian is now called. Mt. Tas, which the inscription mentions as the starting-point of the canal and describes as "a difficult mountain on the border of Urarṭu (Armenia)," can of course not be the cliffs around Bavian, as is usually assumed, but is clearly to be identified with the mountain range where the Atrush rises. The name of the Kurdish clan now inhabiting this district is Doski, which, if we disregard the affix *-ki*, would seem to have preserved as Dos the old name Tas.

To this canal were added the waters of the three villages Me. . . . , Kukkut, and Bīturra. From the context it is not clear whether three different tributaries are meant, one from each village, or one tributary passing all three villages. If the latter is the case, we may compare the modern villages of Meirina, Kan-i-Koka, and Beidul, which range themselves along one of the chief tributaries of the Atrush in just the same order as that in which Me. . . . , Kukkut, and Bīturra occur in the inscription.

The identification of Sennacherib's canal from Mt. Tas with the Atrush leaves one point unexplained, namely the statement that its waters eventually joined those of the Khosr. Since we know that the canal had its outlet at Bavian, in order to reconcile the two statements we must suppose that at Bavian it joined the Khosr system. In fact, we must assume that there existed already an older canal connecting Bavian with the Khosr, so that the waters of the new Atrush canal could be carried down to that river.

Fortunately the existence of such a connection need not be left to pure deduction from texts, for the remains of it still exist and we were able to trace its course (see pp. 29–30). There is no reference to it in the Bavian inscription because it was not contemporary with the Atrush canal but earlier.

This contention is proved by a comparison of the standard inscription of the Jerwan aqueduct with the Bavian inscription. In the Bavian inscription it is stated that the old name of the present Atrush River was changed to Sennacherib's Channel when the river was canalized. Now this old name, which unfortunately has been broken away in the Bavian inscription, is apparently preserved in the inscription of the Jerwan aqueduct, for there we read that the canal to which the aqueduct belonged fed from a river called Pulpullia (see pp. 20–22). Since the Jerwan canal—as can be proved on the ground—actually fed from the present Gomel-Atrush at a point near the rock sculptures of Bavian, and since the first tributary to the Jerwan canal was the "waters of Ḫanusa," which can be identified with certainty as the modern brook of Ḫines, joining the Gomel-Atrush less than one kilometer below the rock sculptures, there can be no doubt whatever that the name Pulpullia refers to the Gomel-Atrush. We have thus in the inscriptions not only the name Sennacherib's Channel for the Gomel-Atrush, but also the name Pulpullia. It seems, therefore, an obvious conclusion that Pulpullia is that river's old name, which according to the Bavian inscription was changed into Sennacherib's Channel. Now we may argue that had the Jerwan inscription been written at the same time as or later than the Bavian inscription the scribe would have been certain to use the flattering name Sennacherib's Channel for the Atrush, whereas instead he uses the older name. Thus we may conclude that he wrote before the Atrush was renamed; in other words, the Bavian-Khosr canal must be earlier than the canalization of the Atrush River.

It remains to add a few words concerning the transfer of the waters of the Atrush canal to the canal below Bavian. The Bavian inscription states that the Atrush canal had sluices. The only point at which we should expect to find sluices is where the Atrush met the older, artificial canal, namely at Bavian; for the Atrush, although canalized, would of course still carry an amount of water varying according to season. By placing sluices at this point, however, it would be possible to regulate conveniently the amount transferred to the artificial canal and thus to the Khosr.

The exact details of how the transfer was arranged are of course unknown to us, but it seems likely that Sennacherib's method would not vary much from the modern practice of the peasants in this region. This consists of damming the river with a fixed weir placed obliquely across the stream to a height which allows superfluous water to pass over it. An outlet into the canal is made from a corner of the lake thus formed. Now the gorge at Bavian widens for a short distance a little below the sculptures, thus forming a natural reservoir. The southern outlet of this reservoir suggests itself as the obvious place for such a weir, and at just this point there is on the right bank of the Gomel a long artificial cleft, 7 meters wide, cut into the cliff (Pl. XXXI*B*). This cleft may well have been the conduit from the reservoir into the canal, and here we may expect the sluice gates to have been situated.[50] A further investigation of the gorge with this problem in mind might produce interesting results.

[50] Cf. p. 30 and see especially the new evidence in chap. vi, obtained after the lines above were written.

VI

THE CANAL HEAD AT BAVIAN

The interesting problem of the arrangement of reservoir and sluices in the Bavian gorge for the feeding of the Bavian-Khosr canal was mentioned at the conclusion of chapter v. This problem we had determined to investigate further; and accordingly in the spring of 1934 arrangements were made for the Jerwan party of the previous year to return and resume work for a fortnight in the neighborhood of the gorge. Quarters were found in the village of Ḫines,[1] since Bavian, which gives its name to the rock sculptures, is situated some way down the Gomel River.

The object we had in view was to identify the ancient remains in this locality, which have in the past been successively investigated and described by A. H. Layard,[2] L. W. King,[3] and W. Bachmann,[4] and re-examine them in the light of our new knowledge of Sennacherib's canal system and its connection with the Gomel River at the point in question. This we proceeded to do as thoroughly as the time at our disposal would permit. In addition to this Dr. Jacobsen was able to repeat the acrobatic feats of several of our predecessors at Bavian and obtain access by a rope to the cliff face, where he collated the more important inscriptions (Pl. XXXII).[5] Also a new survey was made of the valley to fix the positions of the various sculptures and to illustrate our new theories in connection with the restoration of these and other remains. We had come prepared to undertake a small amount of excavation, and this at once proved necessary in order to confirm certain of these theories.

A glance at the sketch map (Fig. 10) gives one a further idea of the character of the gorge described by Dr. Jacobsen on page 43. The mountain pass widens into a valley, inclosed by precipitous cliffs, through which the Gomel flows in a southerly direction until the rocks converge again so that the river passes out into the open country beyond through a narrow defile (see Pl. XIII). At one point (*R* in Fig. 10) it almost washes the base of the western cliffs, and it is here that great fallen sculptures lie half-submerged in a deep pool, while above, in the vertical face of the rock, there appear a number of panels carved with inscriptions and Assyrian figures in relief which have for many generations been known as the "rock sculptures of Bavian" (e.g. Pl. XXXIII). The pathway from Ḫines, which at first follows the west bank of the river, here passes between the latter and the base of the cliff and proceeds to follow a flat shelf of rock (*S* in Fig. 10; cf. Pl. XIII) which slopes steeply upward, turning away from the river, and eventually widens into a sort of grassy amphitheater surrounded on three sides

[1] [To our surprise the village itself yielded a building block of apparently local stone bearing in Hittite hieroglyphs an inscription of a king of Hamath. This will be published in "Oriental Institute Communications," No. 19.—Ed.]

[2] *Discoveries in the Ruins of Nineveh and Babylon*, pp. 207–16.

[3] In Bachmann, *Felsreliefs in Assyrien*, pp. iii–vi.

[4] *Ibid.* pp. 1–22.

[5] [Only the passages dealing with Sennacherib's building activities were collated. The collation gave only minor results:

Line 8 (cf. Luckenbill, *The Annals of Sennacherib*, pp. 79 f.): $^{\bar{a}l}$*ban-ba-ri(!)-na* in *A* (northernmost inscription) and *C* (southernmost inscription).

Line 10: $^{\bar{a}l}$*a-lum-rik-si mē*(A)^{meš} in *A*.

Line 14: *i-ta-tu-šu* and [$^{\bar{a}l}$*me*]-*e(!)*-[illegible] [$^{\bar{a}}$]^{l}*ku-uk*-[illegible] in *A*.

Line 23: *A* seems to read [*a-na*]-*ku i(!)-na šarrāni*$^{meš.ni}$. Can this be a mistake?—Th. J.]

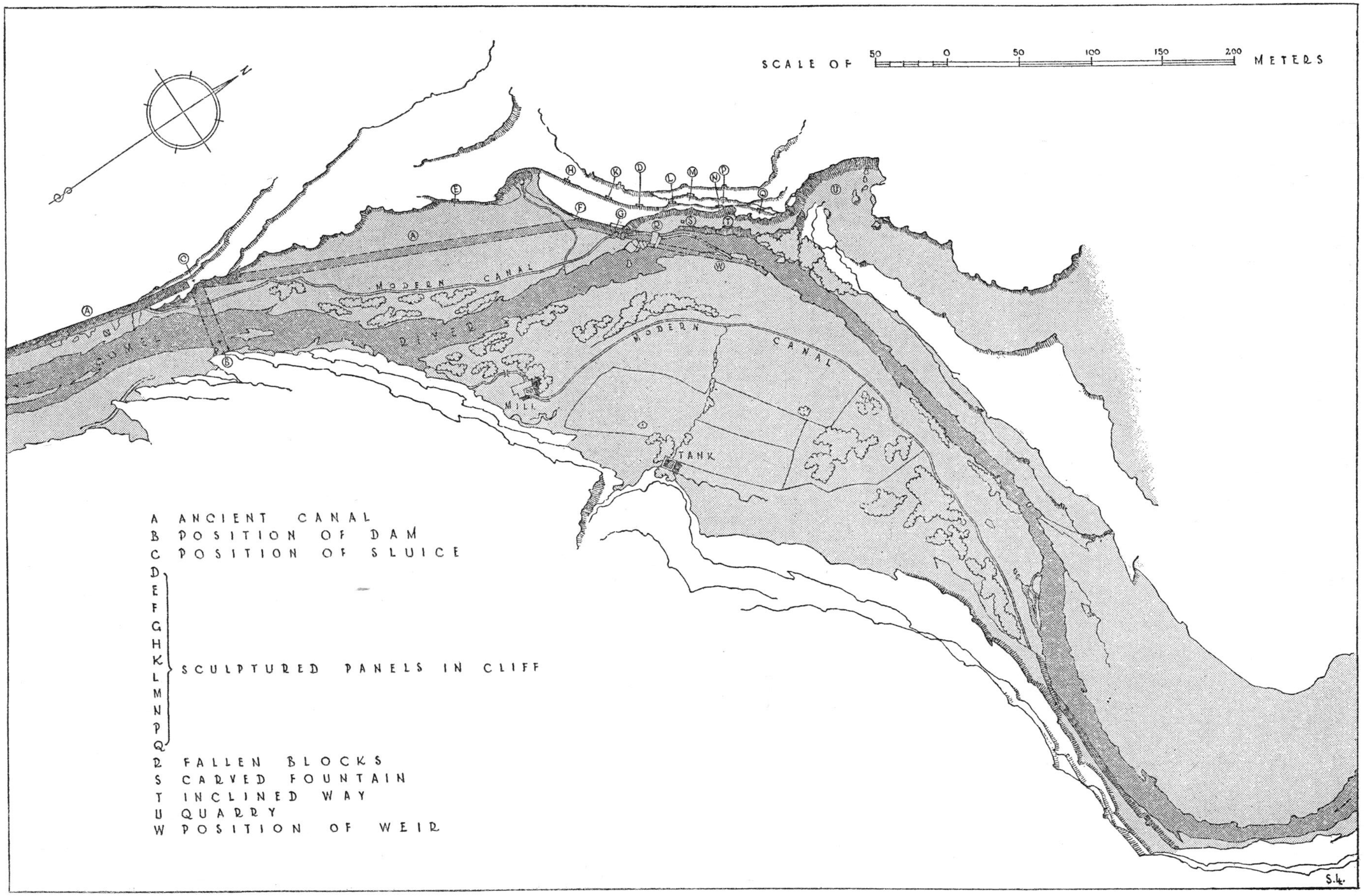

FIG. 10.—SKETCH MAP OF THE GOMEL GORGE, SHOWING COURSE OF ANCIENT CANAL. SCALE, 1:4,000

by vertical walls of limestone (*U* in Fig. 10). Our theory that this is the quarry from which the stone for the canal parapet and the aqueduct was cut was confirmed by matching stone samples from here with fragments from the masonry of the Jerwan structure (cf. p. 13).

It had already been suggested by W. A. Wigram[6] that the natural inclined way mentioned above as giving access to the quarry must have also been used for sliding the blocks of stone down to the river, where they were then mounted on rafts and conveyed by water to their destination. But the depth of the river even in flood time, according to the local villagers, would hardly be adequate for this purpose; and in any case we had previously come to the conclusion that the method of transport used by Sennacherib consisted of rolling or carrying the stones along the dry bed of the canal (see p. 13). This would mean that the head of the canal must have been projected at least as far as the foot of the inclined way, and we therefore considered that a good point at which to begin a careful investigation.

As has already been said, it is here that an enormous block of stone (*R* in Fig. 10) sculptured on its two exposed sides lies, split through the middle and tilted at an angle of about 45° (Pl. XXXIV). On clearing away a quantity of shrubbery we discovered that the underside of this stone rests upon a wall of well preserved masonry, which must have arrested its fall. A few meters to the southwest (near *G* in Fig. 10) we came upon a second, similar face of masonry and found that the base of the cliff opposite the latter was cut artificially to run exactly parallel to it at a distance of 6 meters. Furthermore, this rock face exactly continued the line of the masonry preserved beneath the fallen block.

Here, then, were preserved sections of the two parapets of a canal 6 meters wide apparently connecting with the river at the point where the fallen sculpture lay. Furthermore, there was a modern analogy; for quite recently an elementary dam had been built across the river just above this point (at *W* in Fig. 10), diverting a quantity of water into a small modern irrigation channel which ran beneath the fallen blocks and kept for some distance to the bed of the ancient canal. Farther on, this turned southward, following the line of the river; on reaching the narrow defile at the southwest end of the valley it ran between the river bank and a spur of rock which here comes down to within a short distance of it (see Pl. XXXV).

We saw that there would be no room here (cf. Fig. 11) for an ancient canal 6 meters wide to pass, and accordingly turned our attention to a feature which had interested us on our previous visit and of which Bachmann's explanation seemed to us a little difficult to credit. This consisted of a deep chase (*A* in Fig. 10) cut into the spur of rock mentioned above, stopping abruptly in a vertical face about in the center of the latter (*C* in Fig. 10) but running uninterrupted for some distance to the south along the base of the cliff (see Pl. XXXI*B*). The fact that this cutting measured a little over 6 meters in width confirmed the suspicion we already had that it was the continuation of our canal; and, assuming that for some reason it had been found desirable to tunnel beneath the rock, we proceeded to investigate the north side of the spur for signs of a channel emerging there. Sure enough, after clearing away a growth of oleanders and a quantity of fallen stone, we came upon the same sort of parapet masonry as before butting against the rock face on the east side of what we now took to be the canal. It was not, however, until we began to dig here in earnest (Pl. XXXVI*A*) that we reached first of all the soffit of the tunnel running beneath the rock and then, 2 meters below, the stone floor of the canal.

Meanwhile we had begun digging down at two points into the cutting on the south side of the spur (Pls. XXXI*B* and XXXV). This had in the course of time become filled to the brim with earth and rocks fallen from the hill above, and, partly owing to the restricted space, its excavation proved to be slow work. We managed, however, in the time left to us to

[6] *Cradle of Mankind* (London, 1914) p. 122.

penetrate deep enough to discover in the northwest corner the entrance to a small chamber ($1\times 1\frac{1}{2}\times 2$ meters inside) cut into the vertical face of the rock. We found also a narrow flight of steps (Pl. XXXVI*B*) leading down to the bed of the canal at a point where the latter was about 2 meters beneath the surface (see Fig. 11). Farther south the east side of the canal can be traced by rock cuts with vertical faces (see broken lines in Fig. 11, at left); the gaps between these had evidently been filled with parapets of masonry.

It now only remained to trace the connection between the point at which the canal passed along the base of the cliff beneath the great sculptured panel *G* (Fig. 10) and the point where it ran into the tunnel beneath the rock at *C*. This we were enabled to do by the finding of

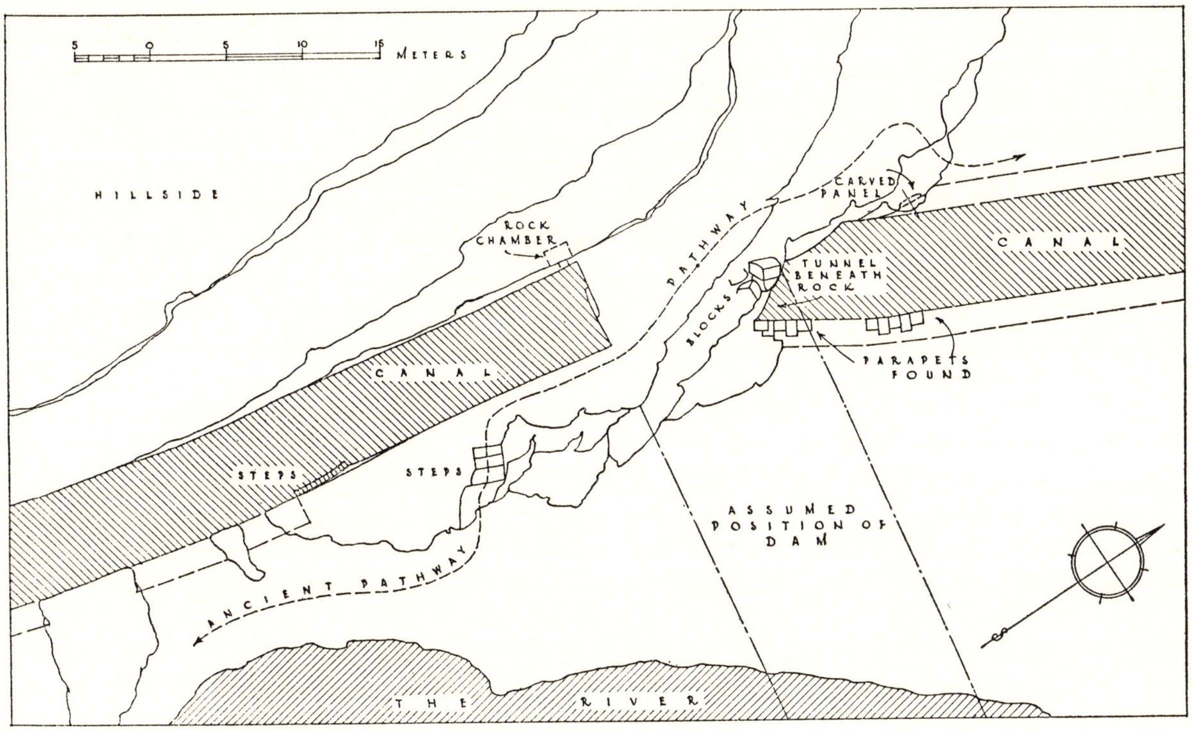

Fig. 11.—Plan of the rock cuttings at the point marked *C* in Figure 10. Scale, 1:500

further traces of the parapets, first at a point about 30 meters northeast of the tunnel, then in the bed of a stream which joins the Gomel a short distance west of the sculptures (beneath *F* in Fig. 10). Thus the whole course of the canal, from the fallen sculptures (*R*) to beyond the southern defile, could now be plotted on our sketch map.

The next problem which presented itself was why a tunnel had been dug at *C* (Fig. 10), whereas it might have involved less labor simply to continue the cutting right across the projecting spur of rock. In observing the contours we at once noticed that this spur occurs at by far the narrowest point in the gorge, a point in fact where the rocks on either side of the river converge to within little more than 50 meters of each other (see Pls. XIII and XXXV). If, therefore, in certain circumstances it was necessary to collect a volume of water to feed the canal by forming a reservoir, here would be the ideal position for a dam; and the tunnel beneath the solid rock would facilitate the construction of sluice gates to regulate the flow of water in the canal. If a dam (*B* in Fig. 10) once existed here, it has now been entirely demolished by successive floods. Only on a ridge above the north entrance to the tunnel are a number of large, roughly shaped blocks which are otherwise difficult to explain. A flight of

INDEX

PRINTED IN U·S·A

SHAIKH ADI

A.—General view

B.—Courtyard near pond with sacred newts

The Yezidi sanctuary at Shaikh Adi

A.—Courtyard

B.—Entrance

PLATE III

One of our Yezidi workmen

An Assyrian (Nestorian) priest and his two deacons visiting ᶜAin Sifni

A.—Laborers from an Arab village

B.—The mukhtar of Jerwan, ᶜAli, in front of his house. Note the inscribed blocks

A.—Fallen blocks in the bed of the stream

B.—The façade, looking toward the central breach

C.—Blocks loosened by settlement

THE JERWAN AQUEDUCT

A.—View from the northwest, with the village

B.—A section of the stone pavement over which the water flowed. View looking west

PLATE VIII

A.—The central breach, seen from the east

B.—The remains of an archway, seen from the south

A.—Remains of parapet and paving, showing a few stones of the tilting course

B.—Types of rustication

C.—Rusticated masonry on the northwest flank

A.—The repaired breach, showing re-used stones inscribed with parts of inscription *D*

B.—The irregular jointing of the repaired portion (on the right)

THE JERWAN AQUEDUCT

A.—An inscribed block (No. 196) occurring behind a facing-block

B.—The remains of two archways, seen from north-northwest, showing blocking (on the right) and semicircular stones from the breakwaters, as found

A.—The corbeling of an archway

B.—The crenelated stones

THE GOMEL GORGE

View looking downstream from quarry on west bank. An inclined way in the foreground descends to the partially submerged sculptures in the center. Beyond the rocks in the distance the valley opens out, and the village of Ḫines is seen toward the right

A.—East end of parapet and pavement, seen from the southeast, showing (in lower right-hand corner) a row of paving stones recessed into those beneath them

B.—Concrete, seen in cross-section

A.—Remains of canal parapet at west end

B.—Inscription *A*, on a surface within the masonry

C.—Cleaning a copy of inscription *B*

THE JERWAN AQUEDUCT

A.—Inscription *B* on the surviving breakwater

B.—Removal of fallen blocks

C.—Inscription *B* as found on the sixth bay

JERWAN INSCRIPTIONS

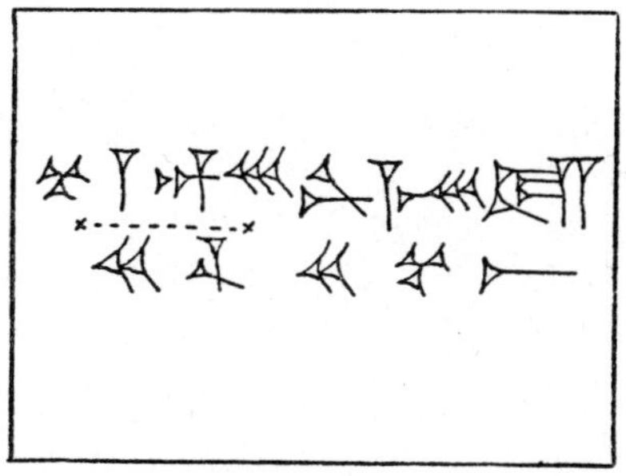

x-----x VAR. OM.

Inscription *A*

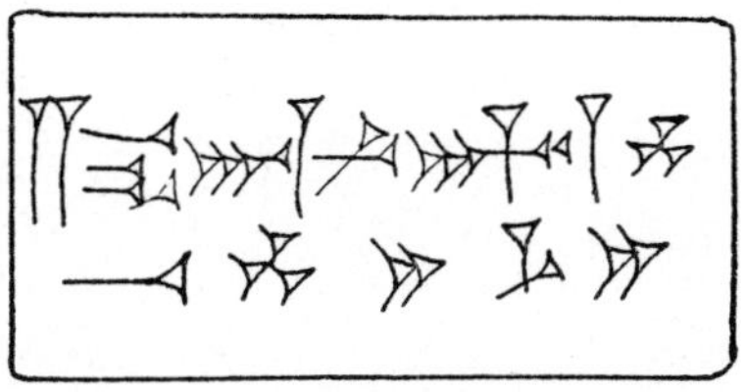

Inscription *A* as found reversed

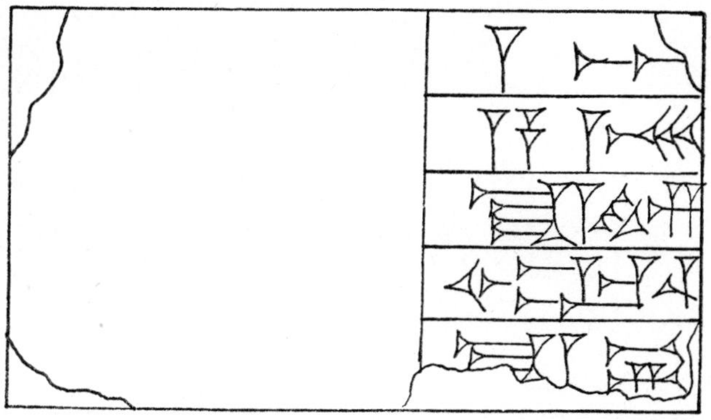

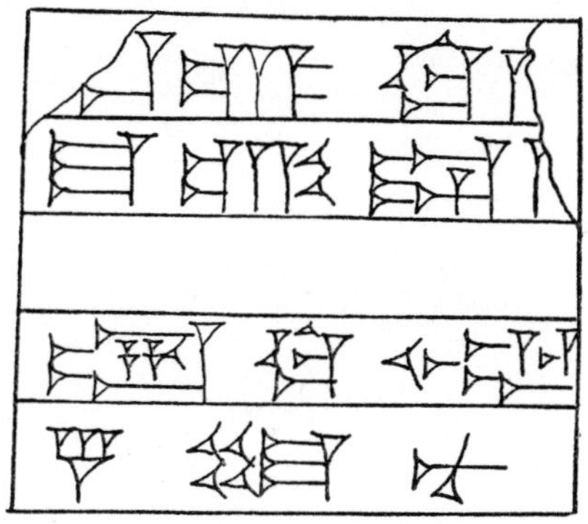

Inscription *B*. Fragments

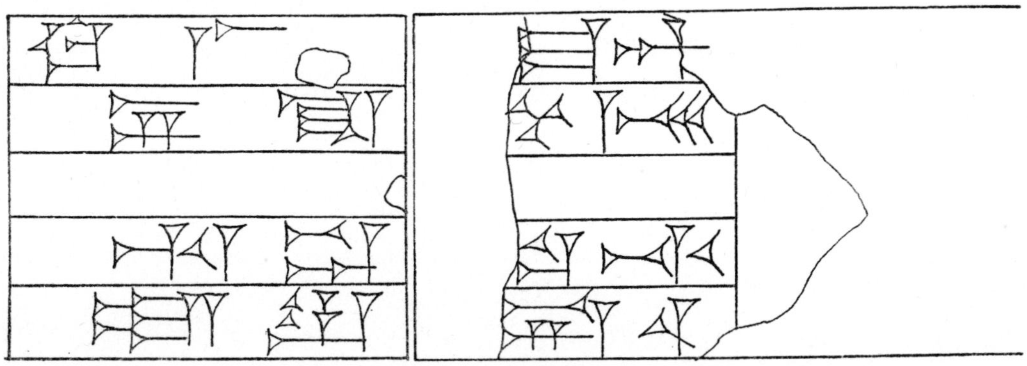

Inscription *B*. Fragments

Facsimiles. Scale, 1:10

JERWAN INSCRIPTIONS

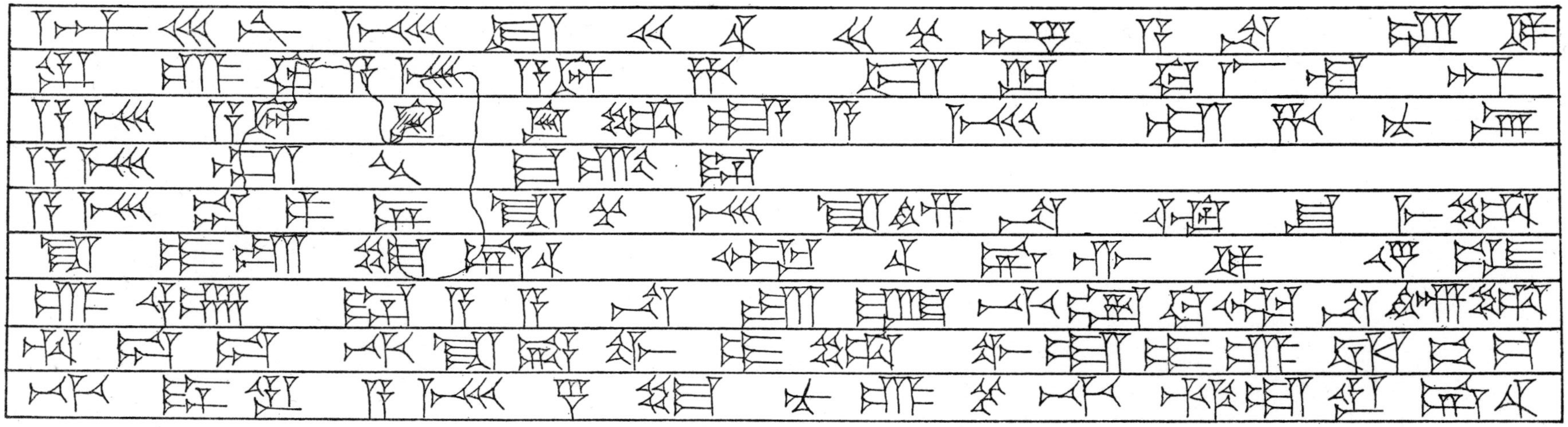

Inscription *B* as found on the sixth bay. Scale, 1:12

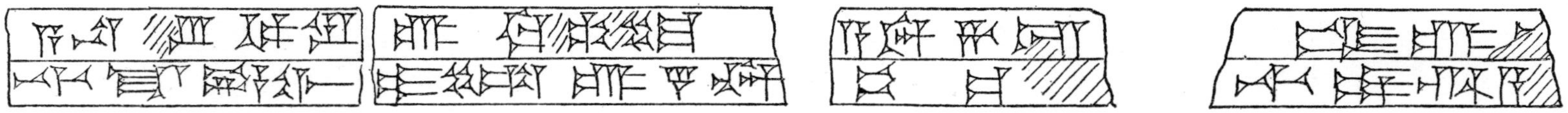

Inscription *C*. Scale, 1:10

Facsimiles

JERWAN INSCRIPTION *D*. PORTIONS FOUND ON RE-USED BLOCKS

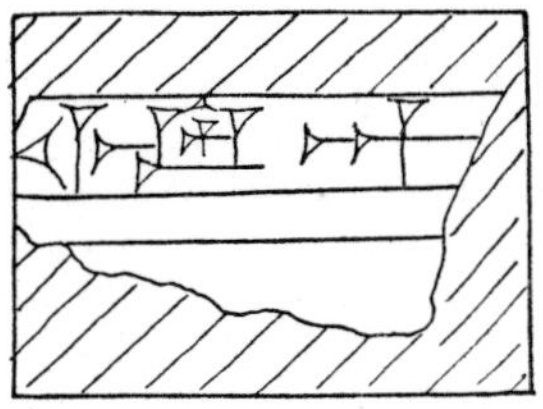

1

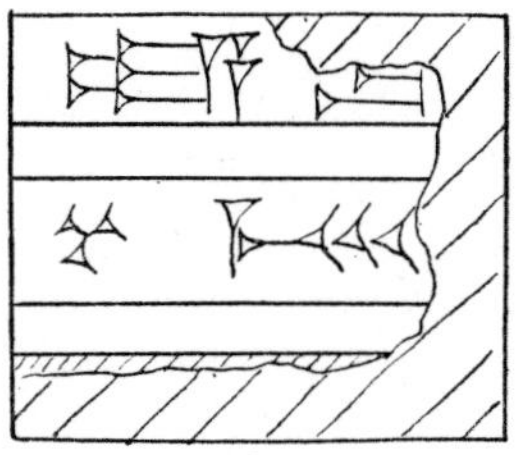

2

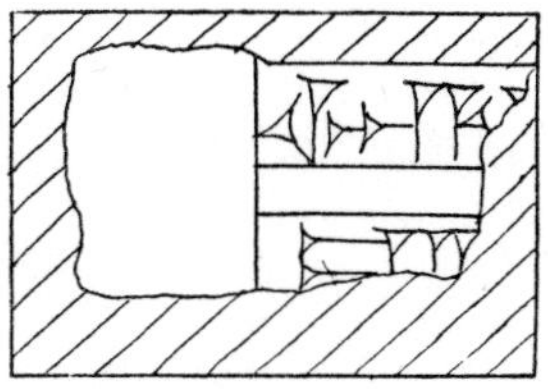

3

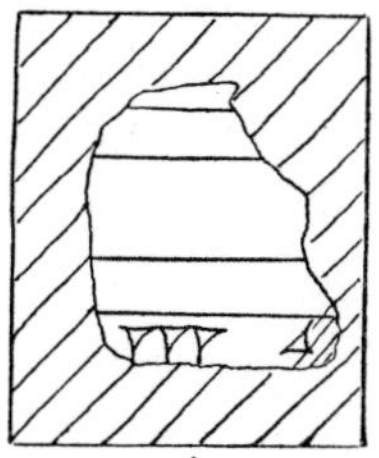

4

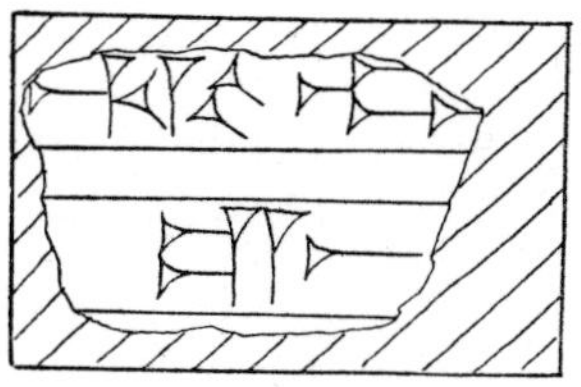

5

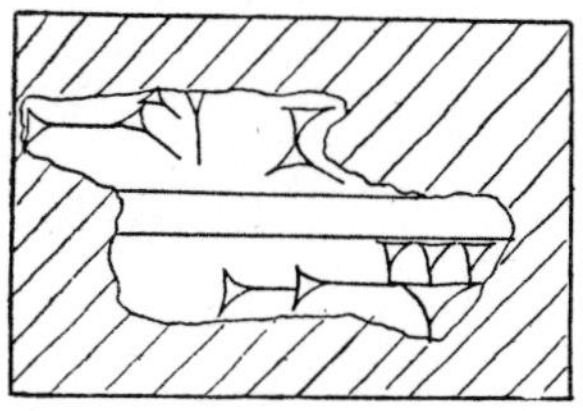

6

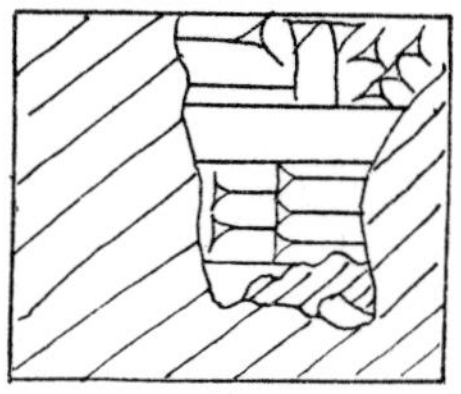

7

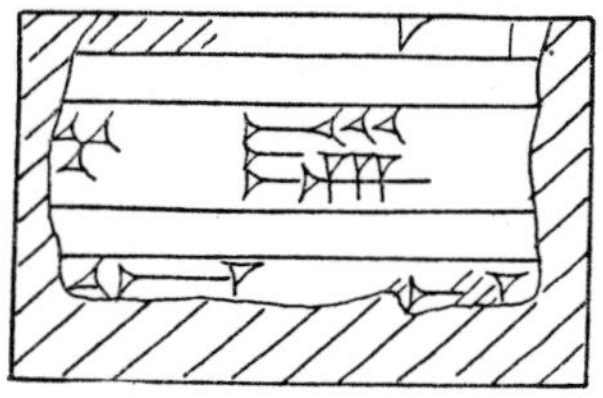

8

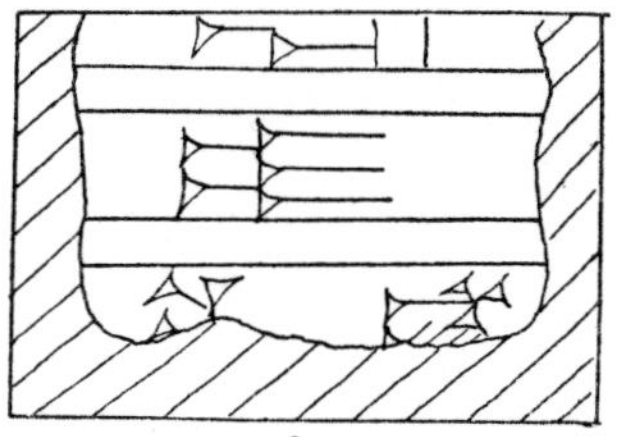

9

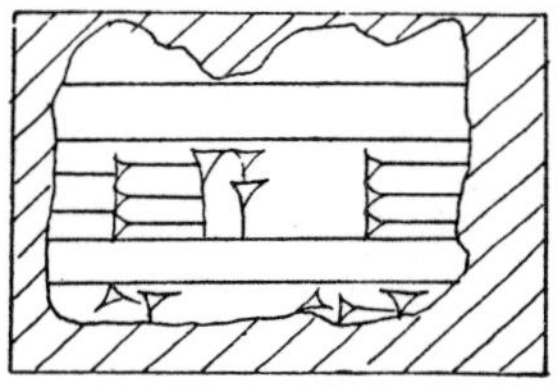

10

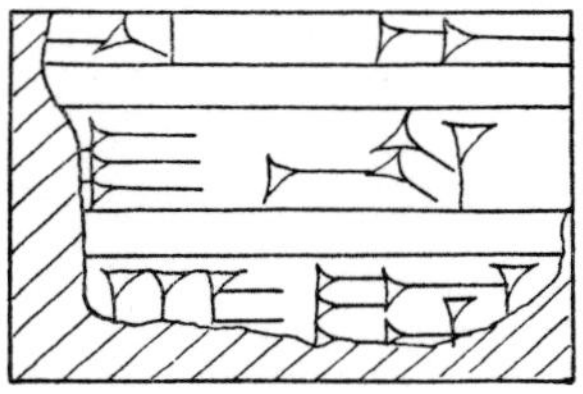

11

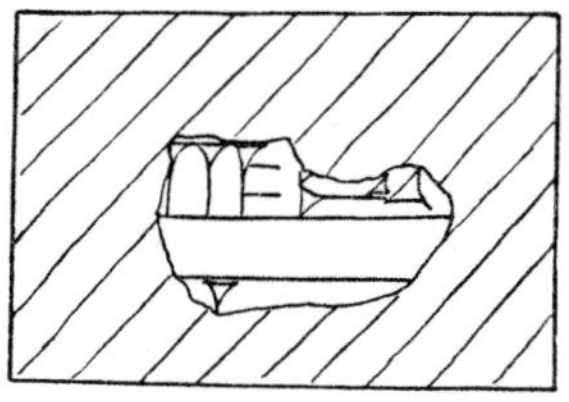

12

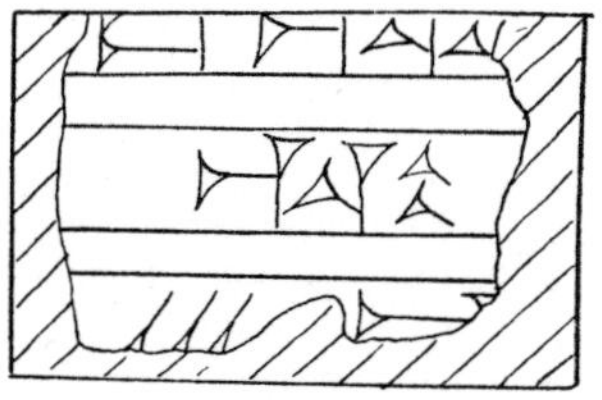

13

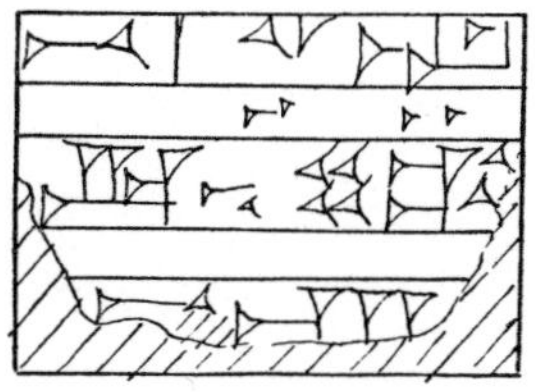

14

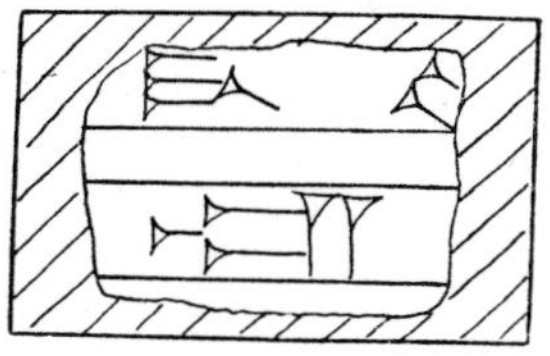

15

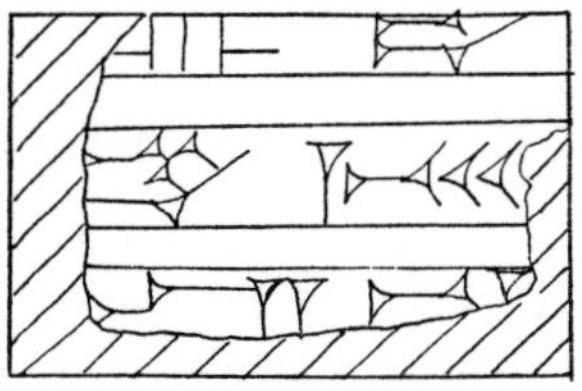

16

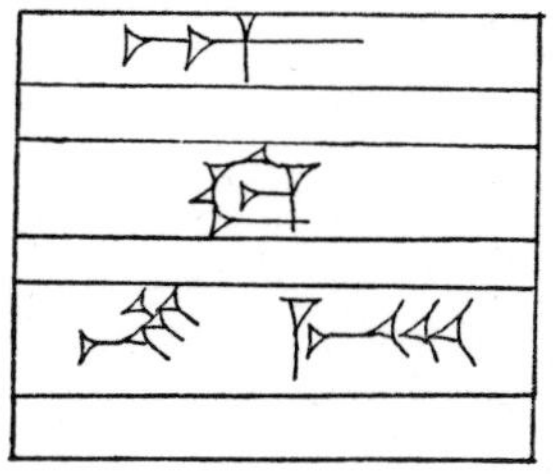

17

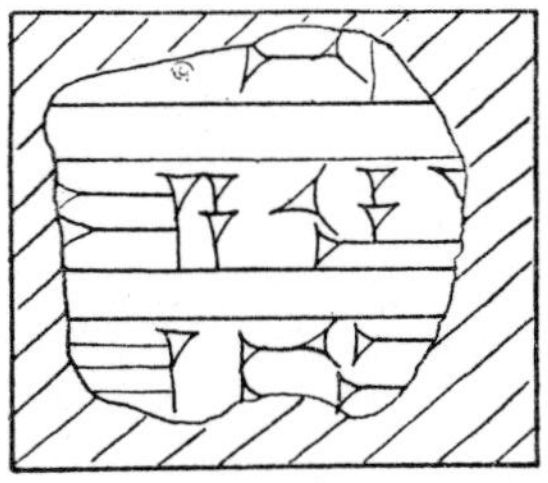

18

Facsimiles. Scale, 1:15

JERWAN INSCRIPTION *D*. PORTIONS FOUND ON RE-USED BLOCKS

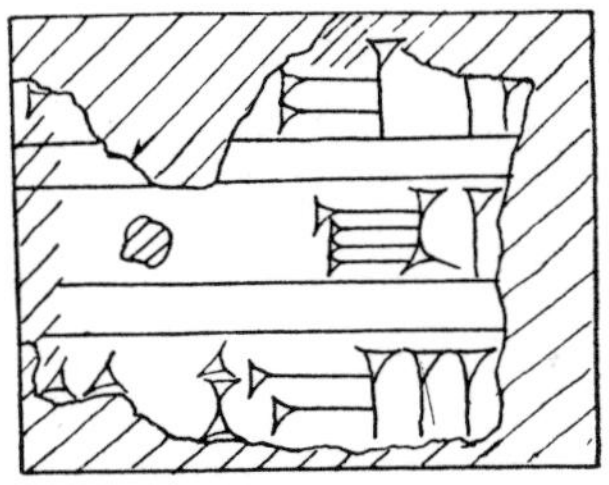
19

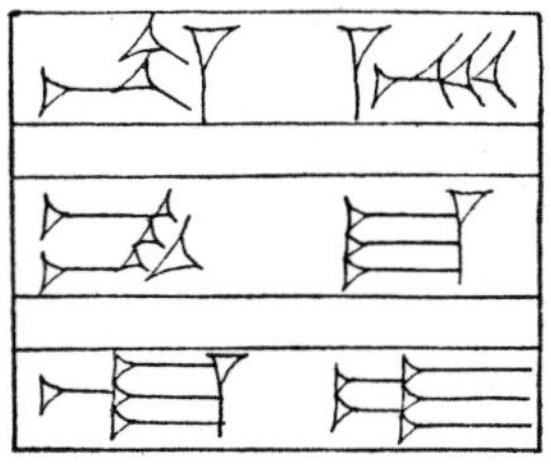
20

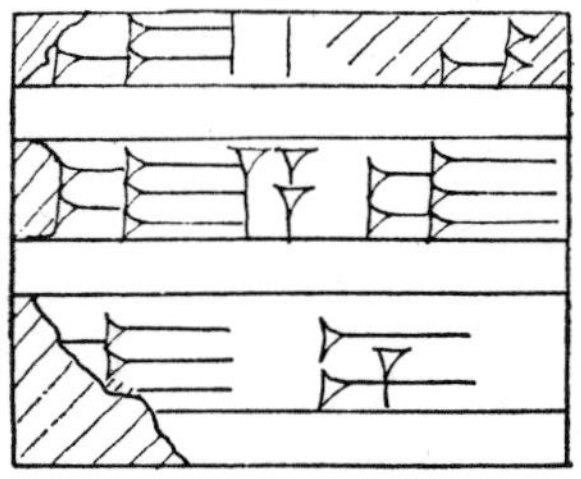
21

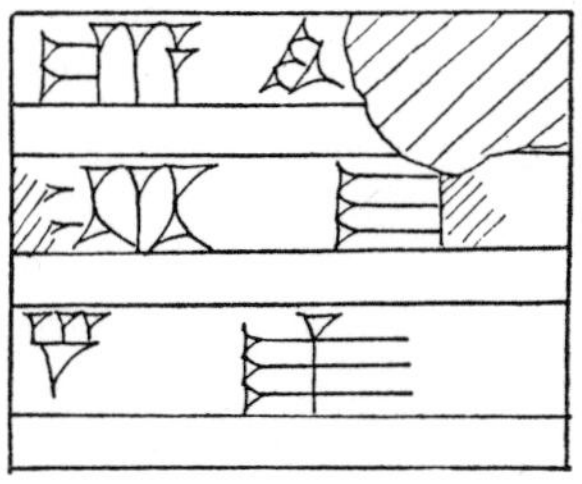
22

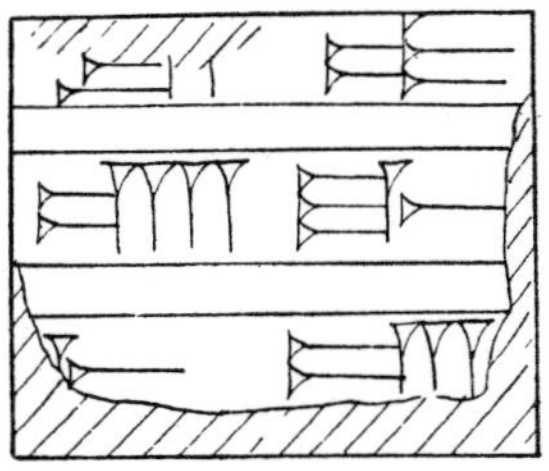
23

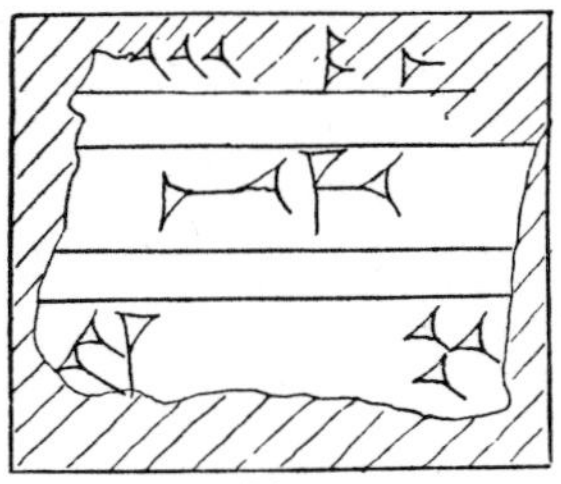
24

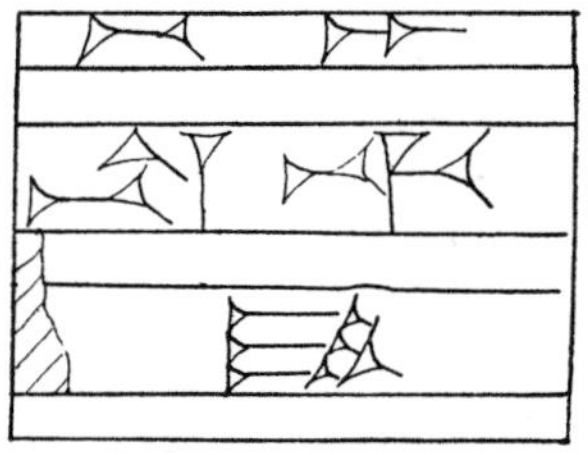
25

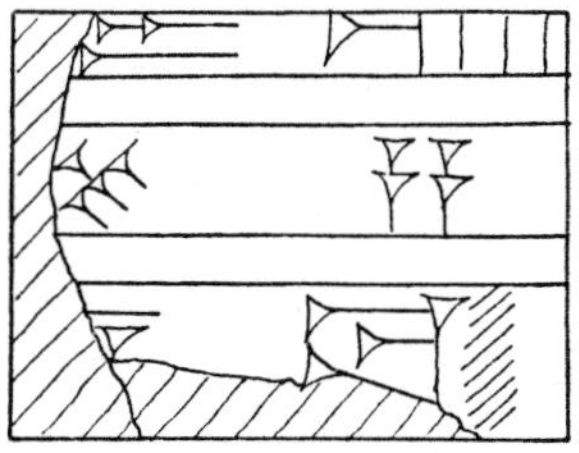
26

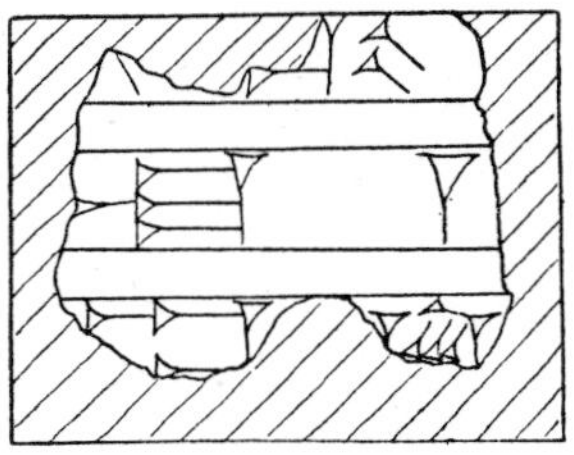
27

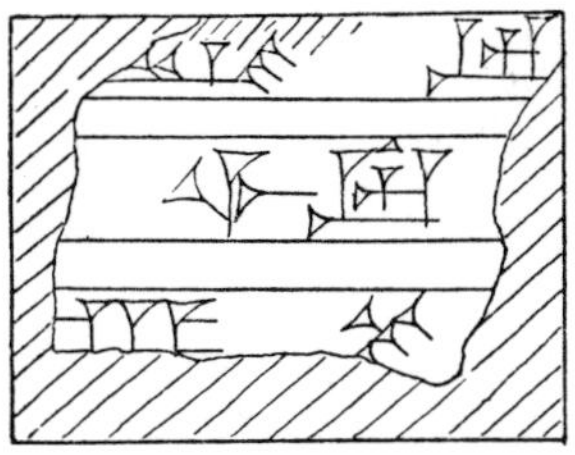
28

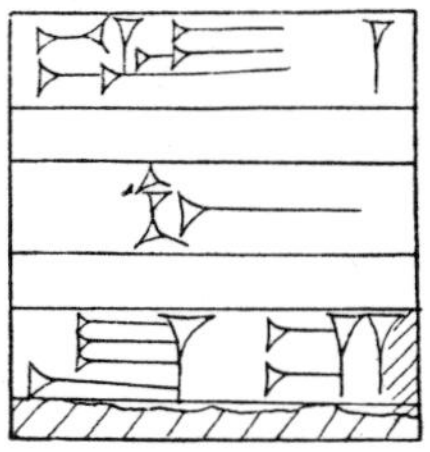
29

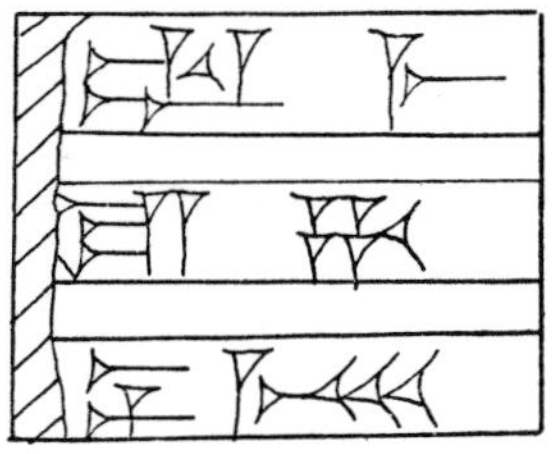
30

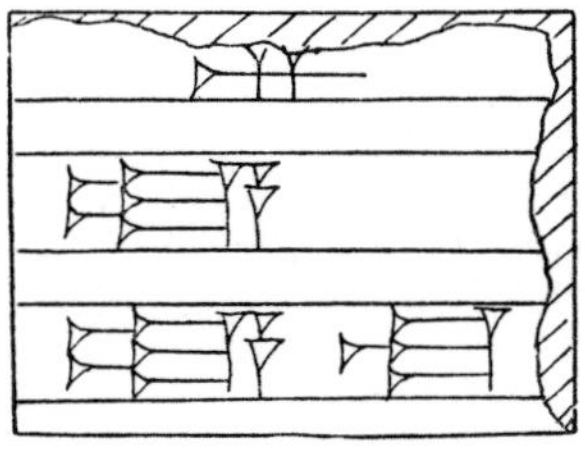
31

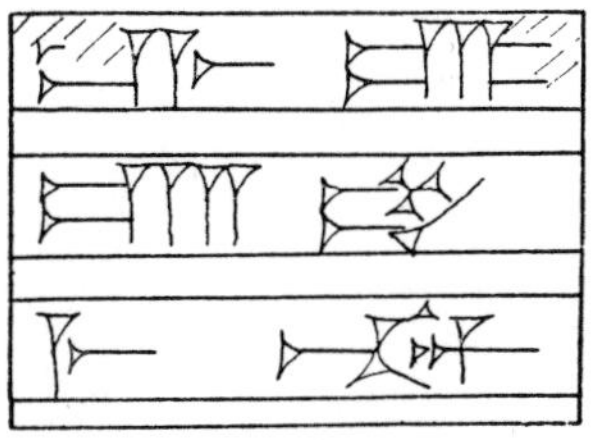
32

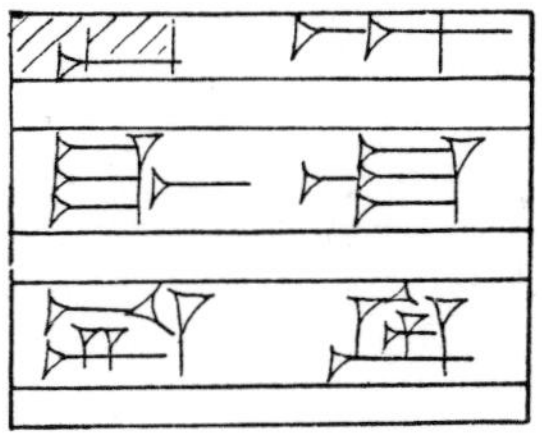
33

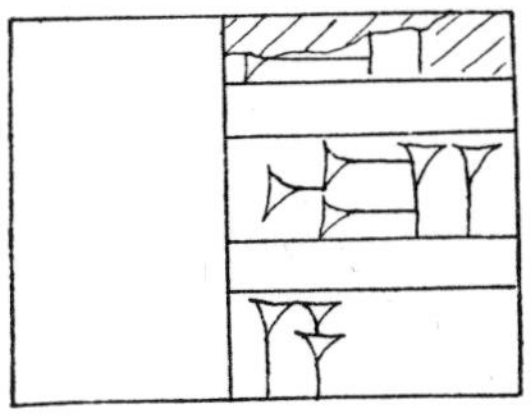
34

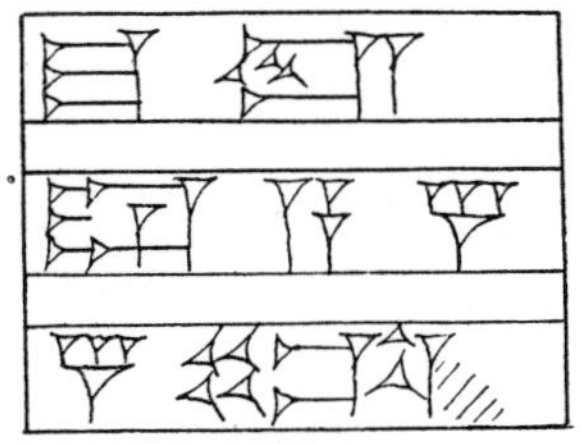
35

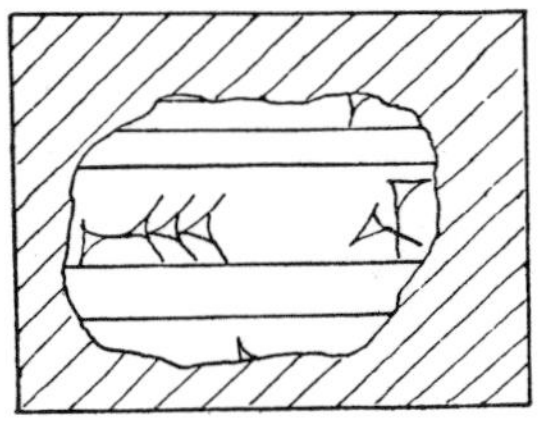
36

Facsimiles. Scale, 1:15

Jerwan inscription *D*. Portions found on re-used blocks

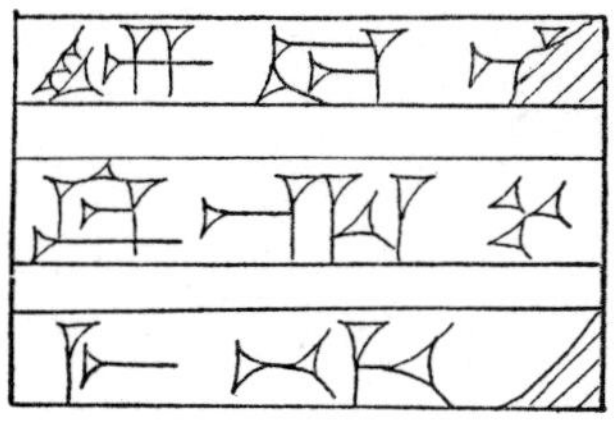
37

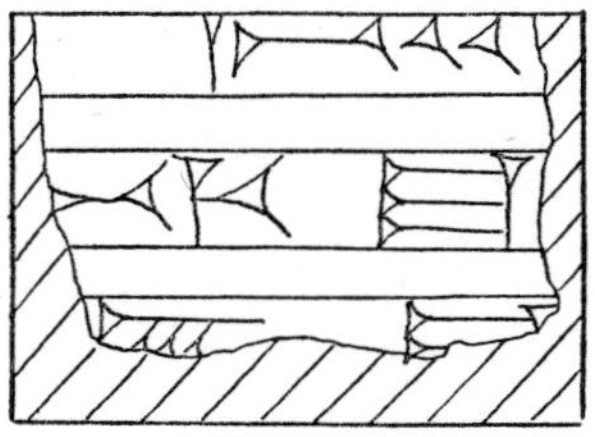
38

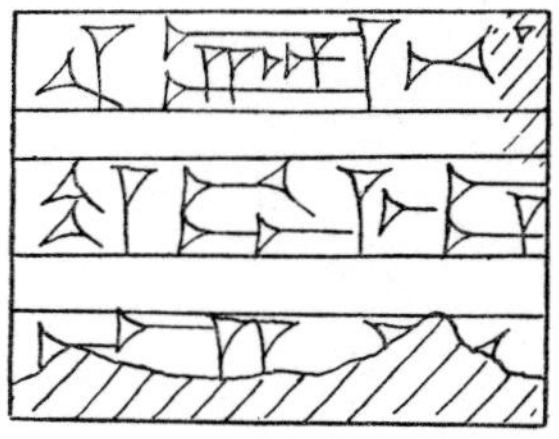
39

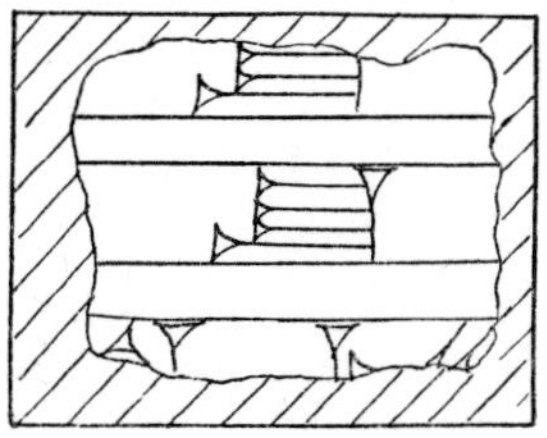
40

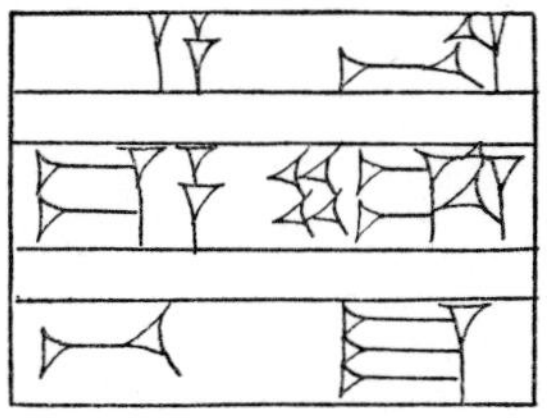
41

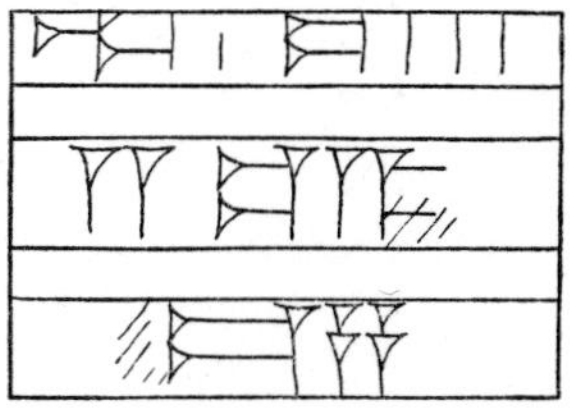
42

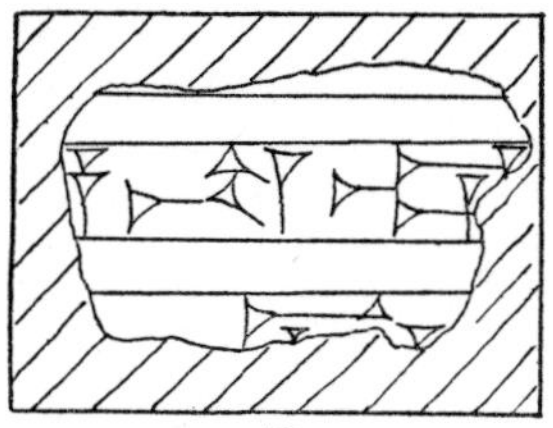
43

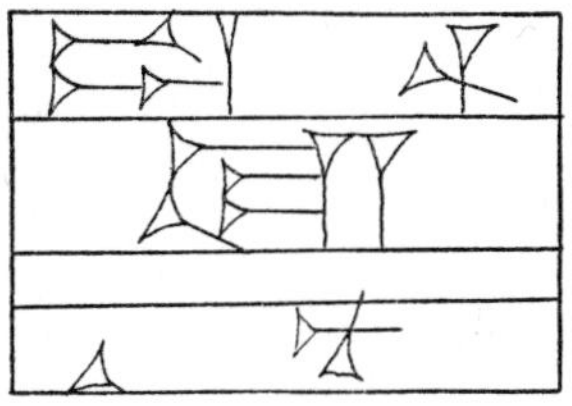
44

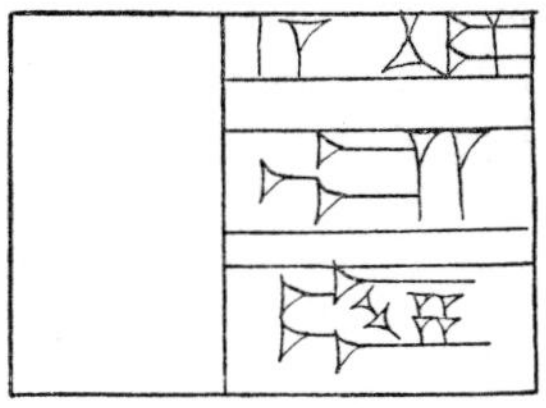
45

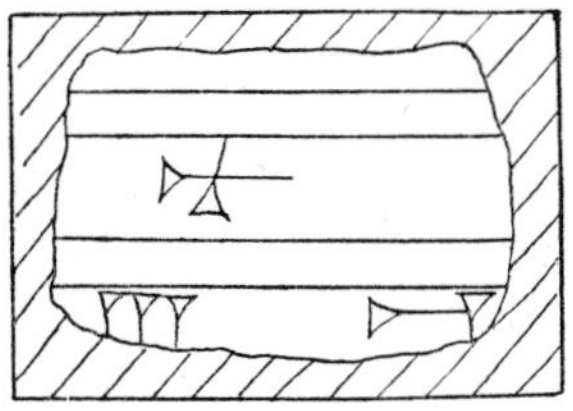
46

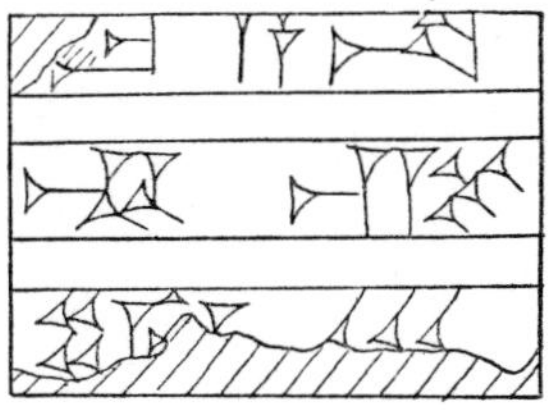
47

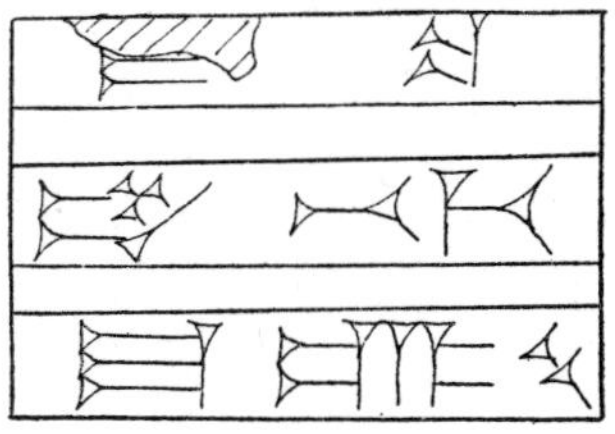
48

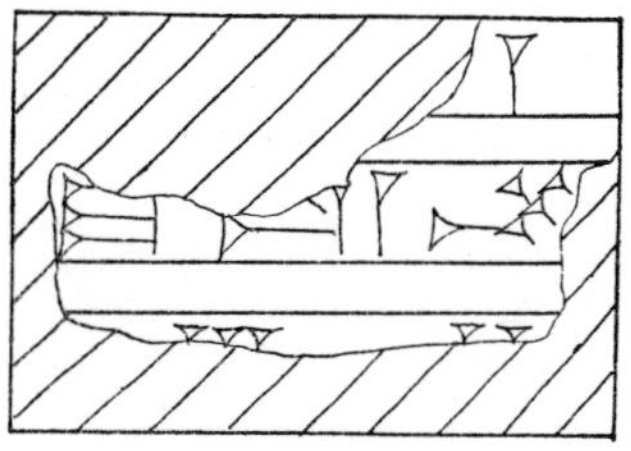
49

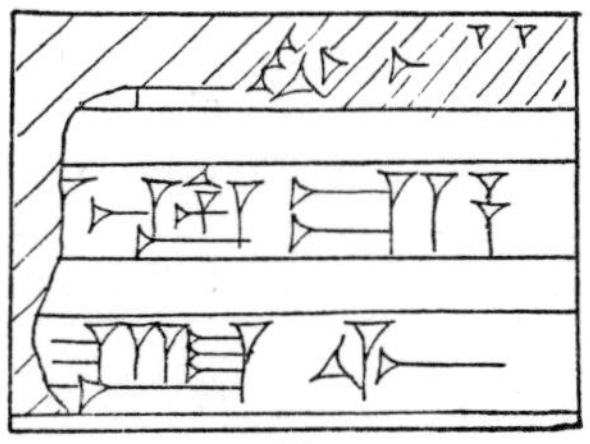
50

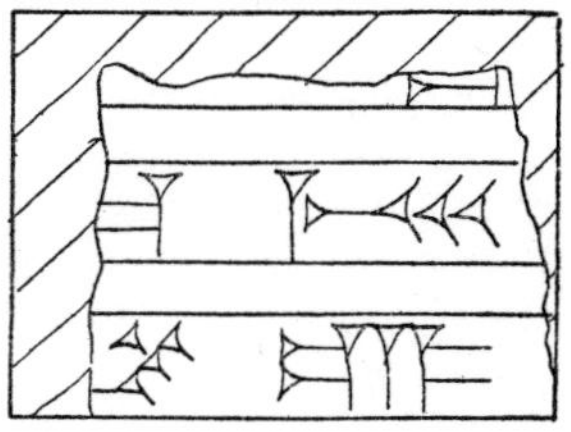
51

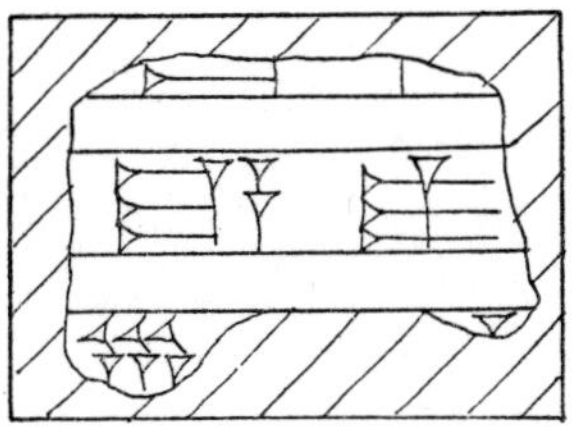
52

53

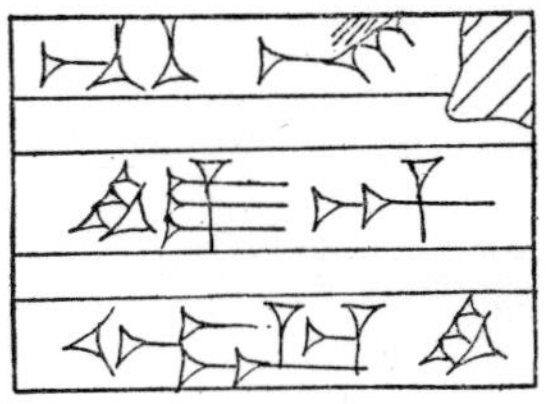
54

Facsimiles. Scale, 1:15

JERWAN INSCRIPTION *D*. PORTIONS FOUND ON RE-USED BLOCKS

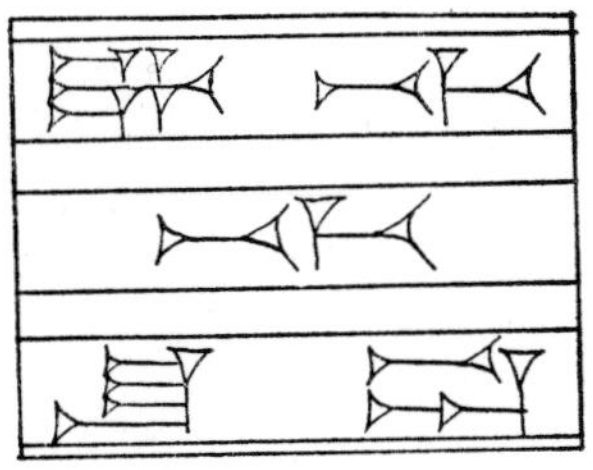

55

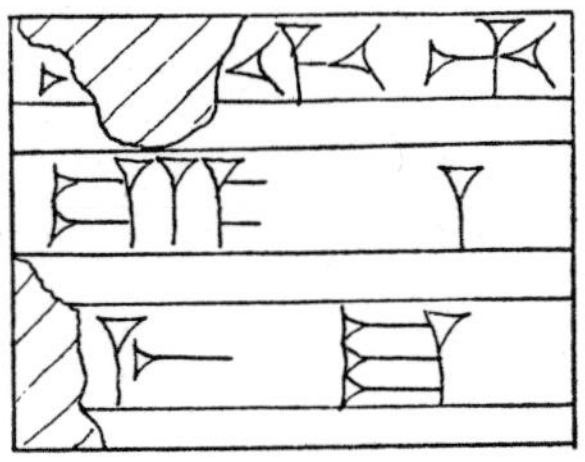

56

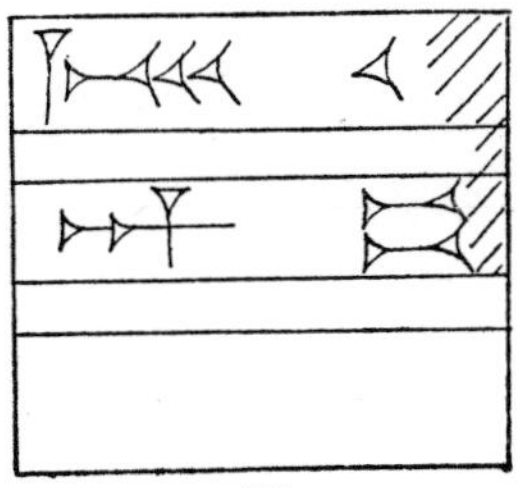

57

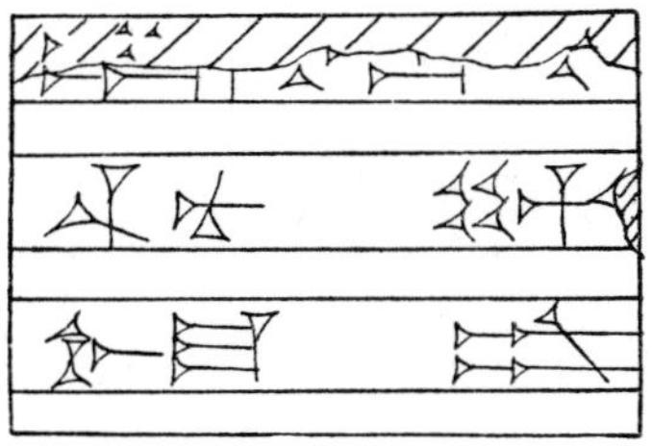

58

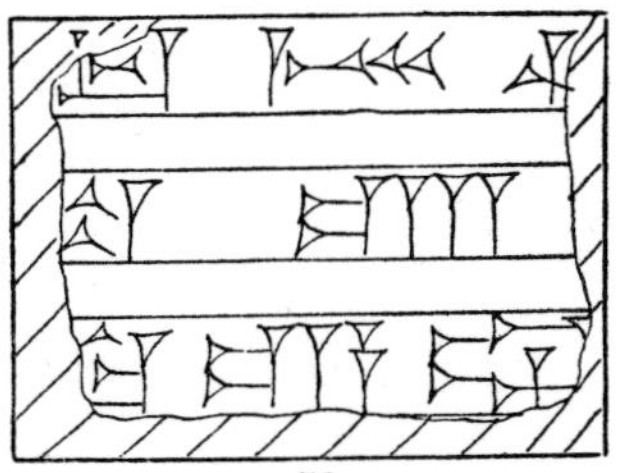

59

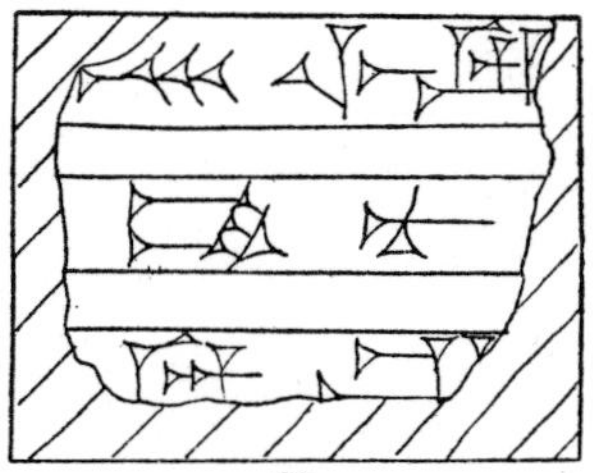

60

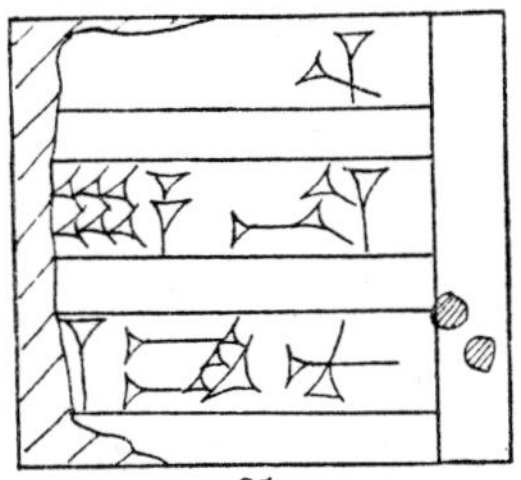

61

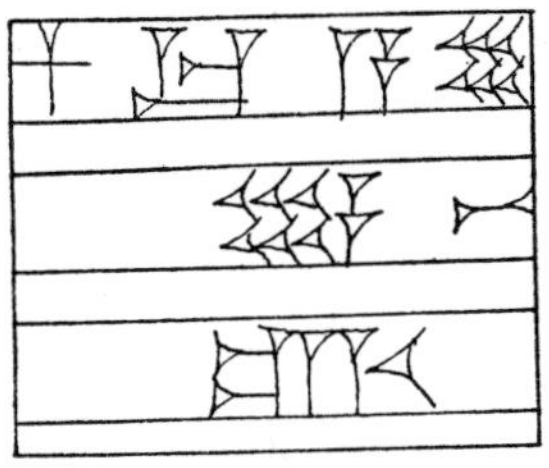

62

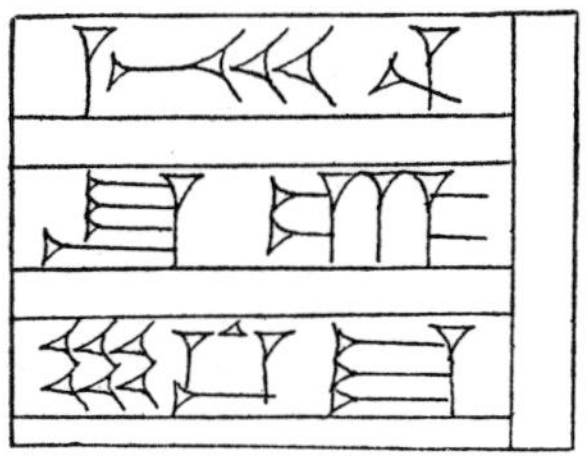

63

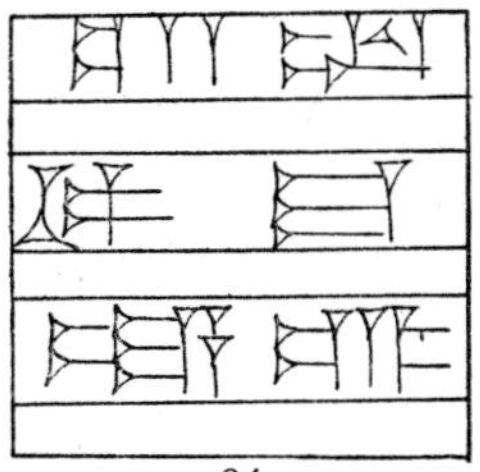

64

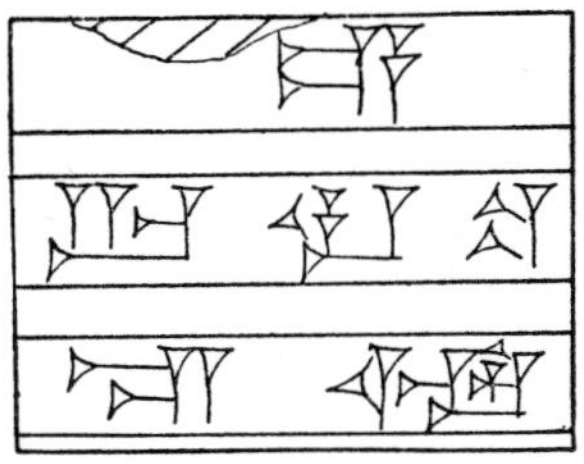

65

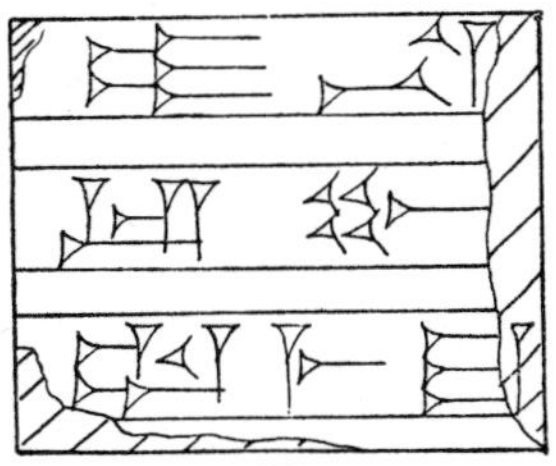

66

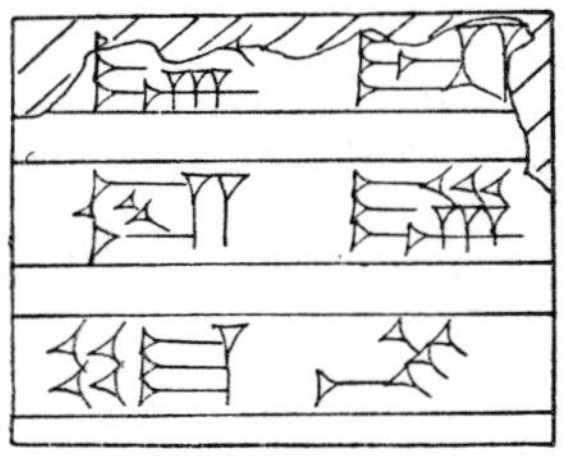

67

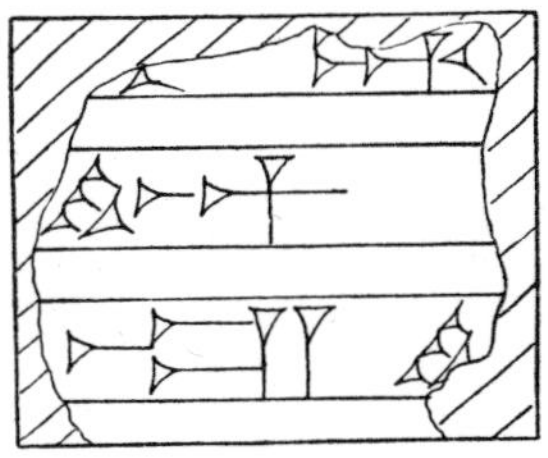

68

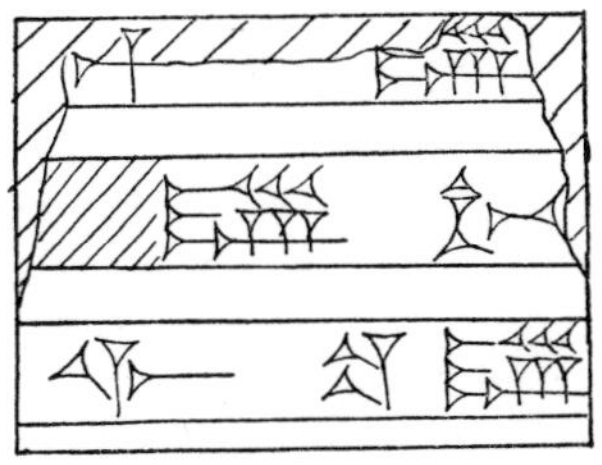

69

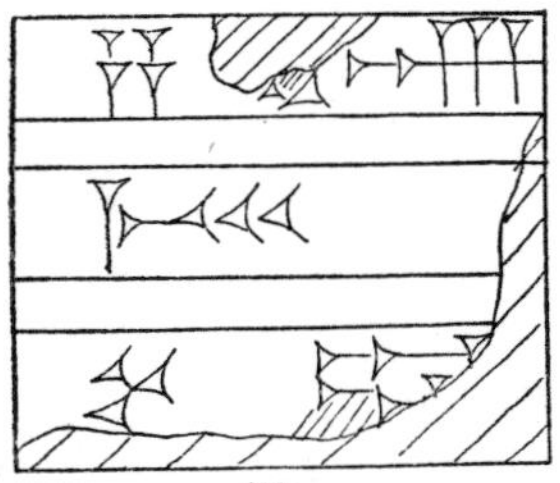

70

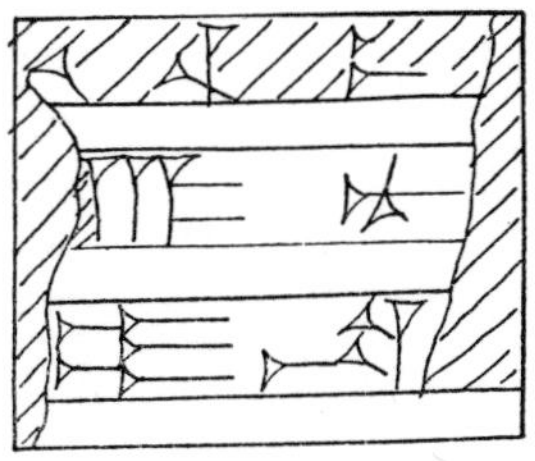

71

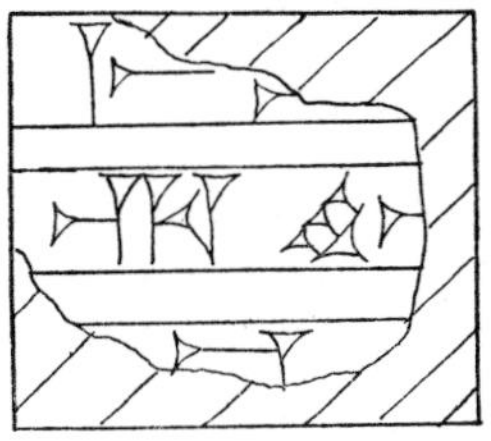

72

Facsimiles. Scale, 1:15

Jerwan inscription *D*. Portions found on re-used blocks

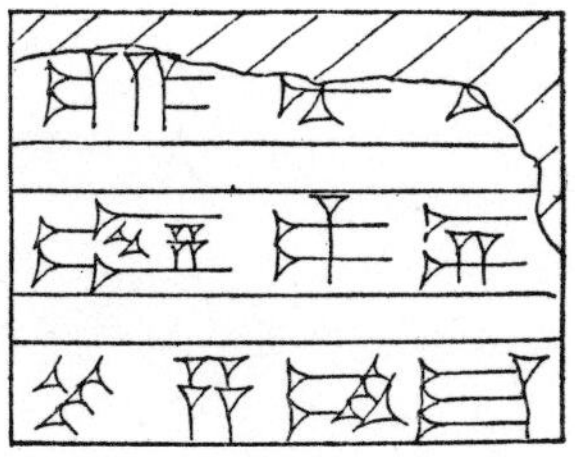

73

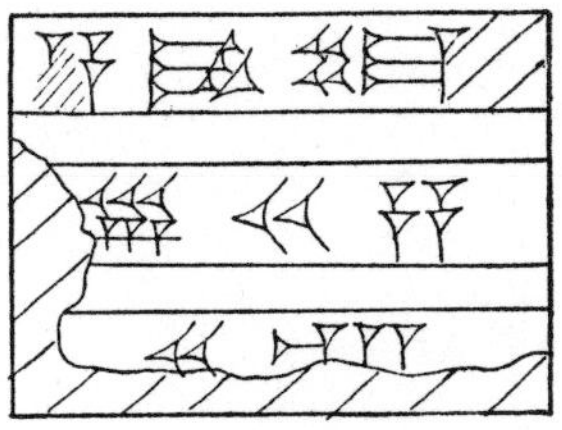

74

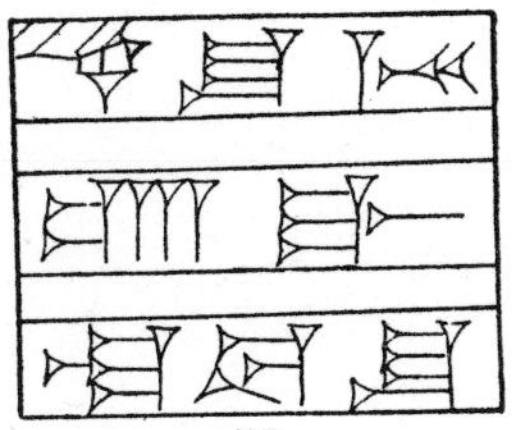

75

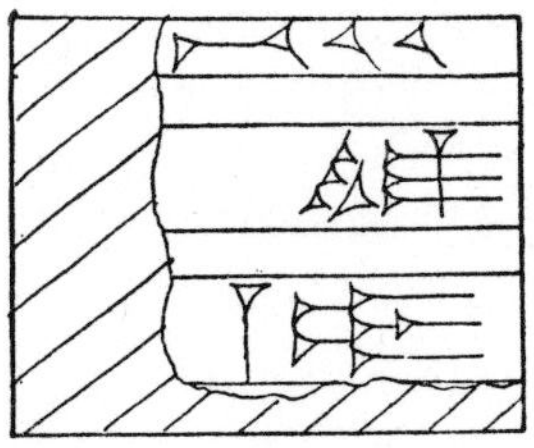

76

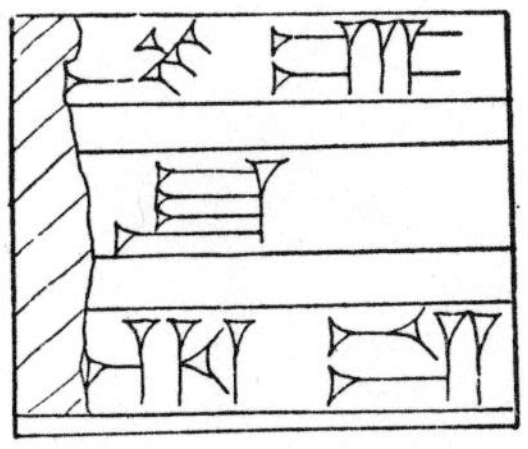

77

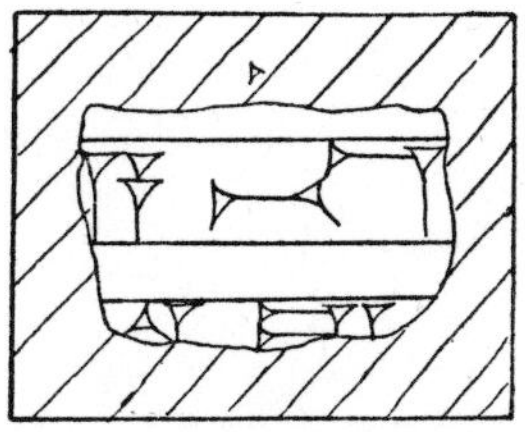

78

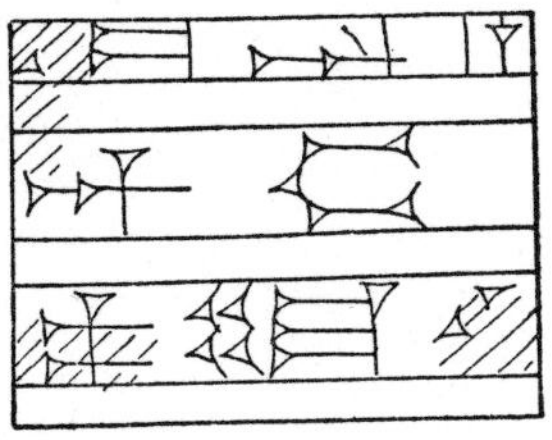

79

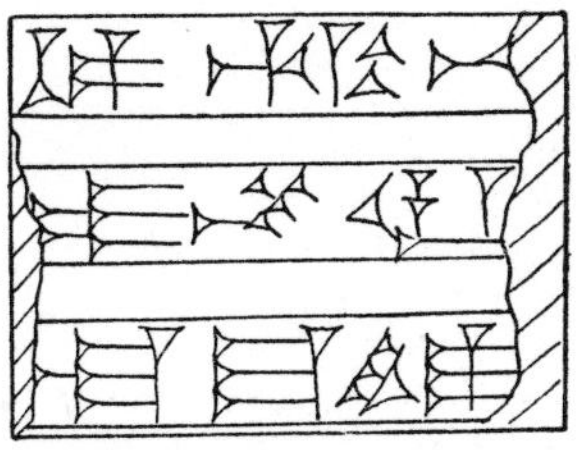

80

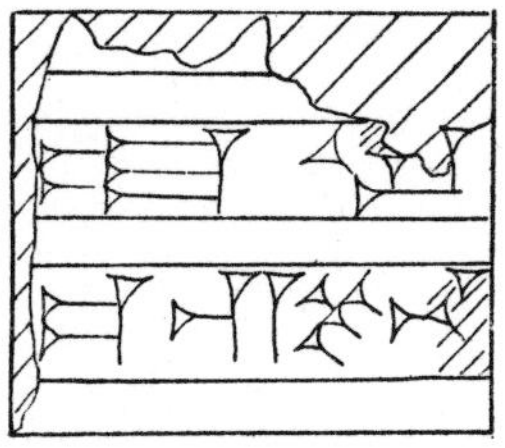

81

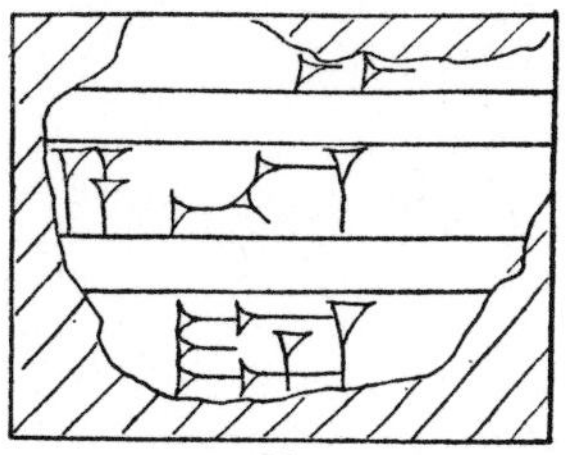

82

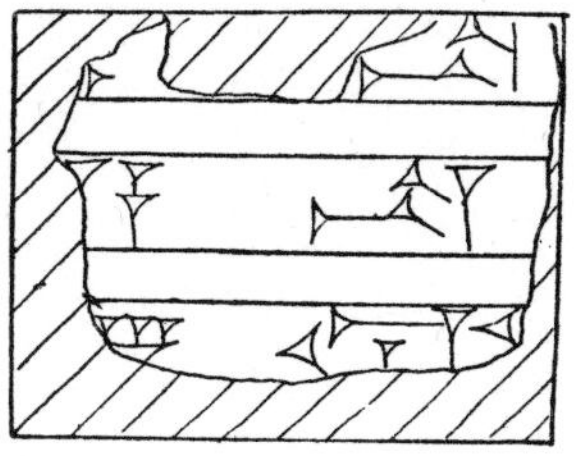

83

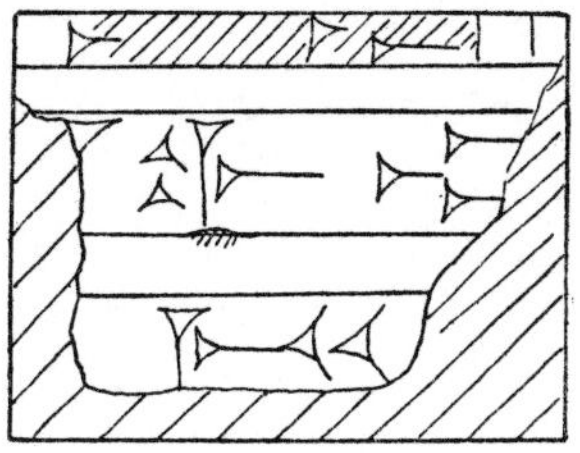

84

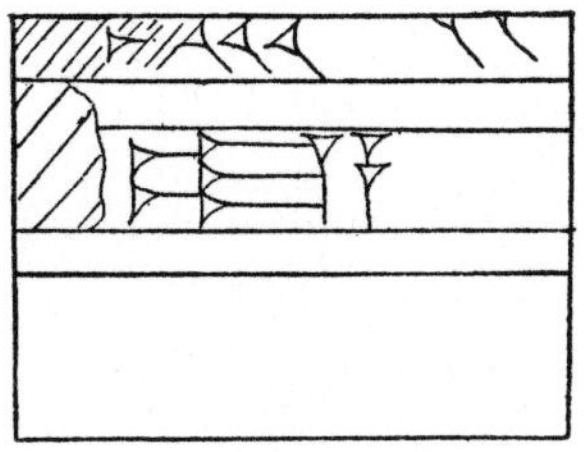

85

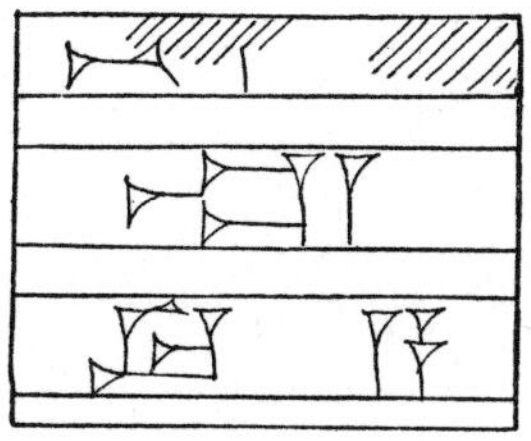

86

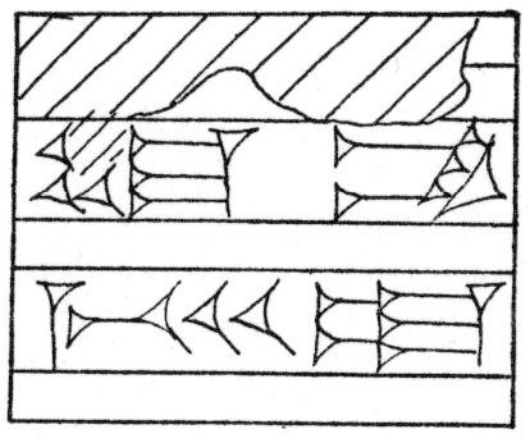

87

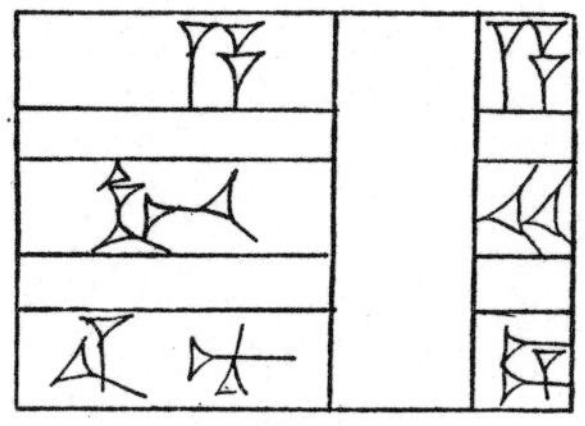

88

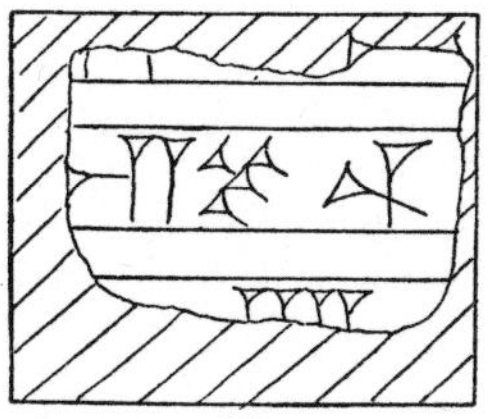

89

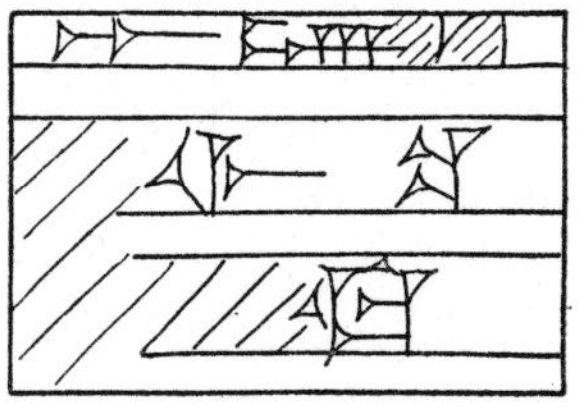

90

Facsimiles. Scale, 1:15

PLATE XXIV

JERWAN INSCRIPTION *D*. PORTIONS FOUND ON RE-USED BLOCKS

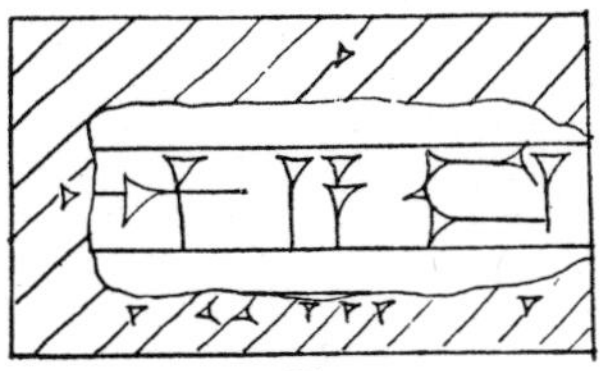
91

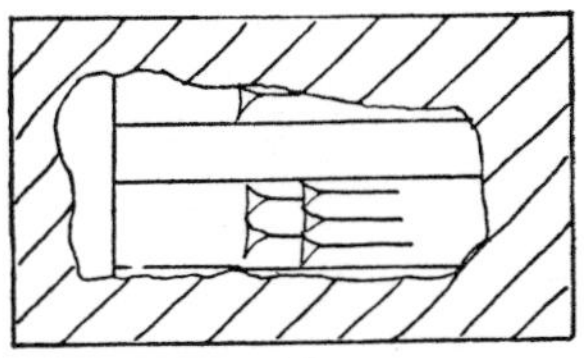
92

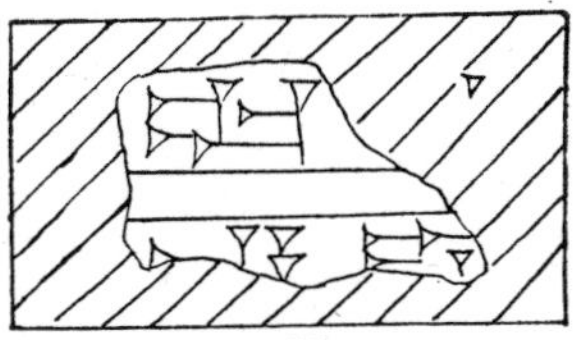
93

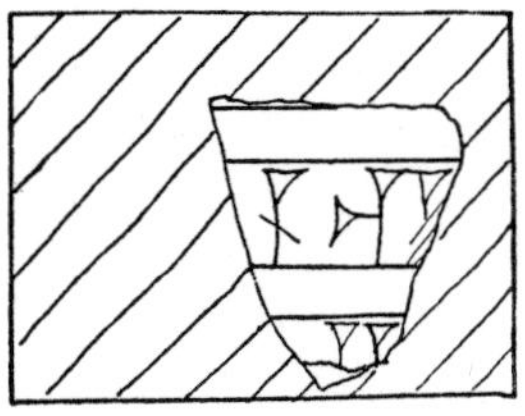
93a

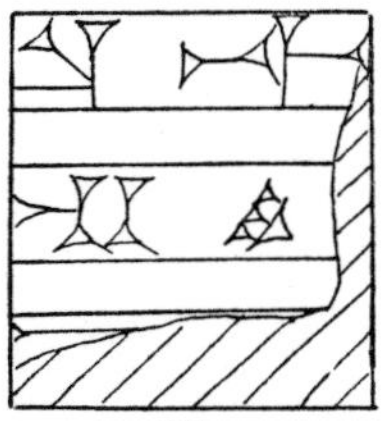
94

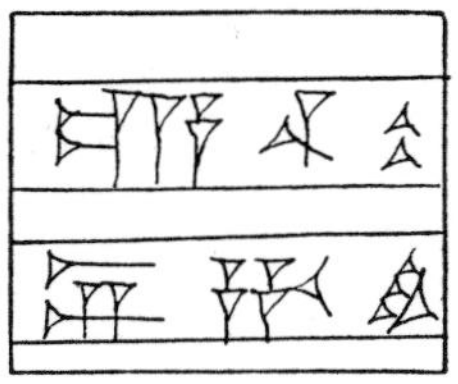
95

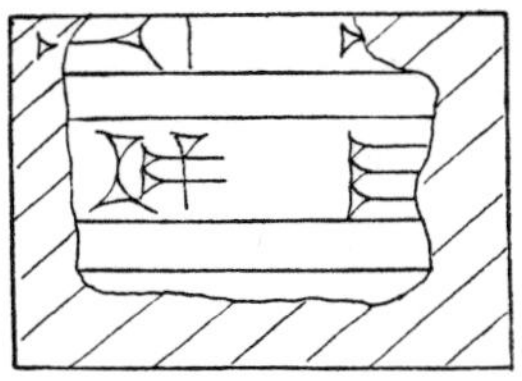
96

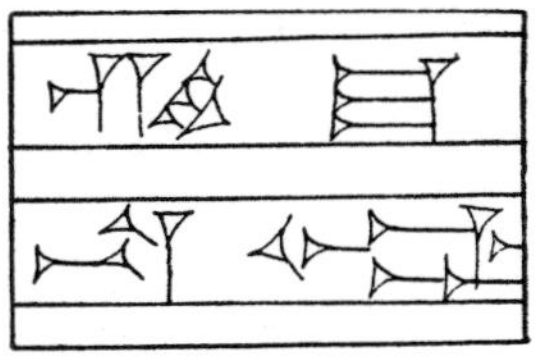
97

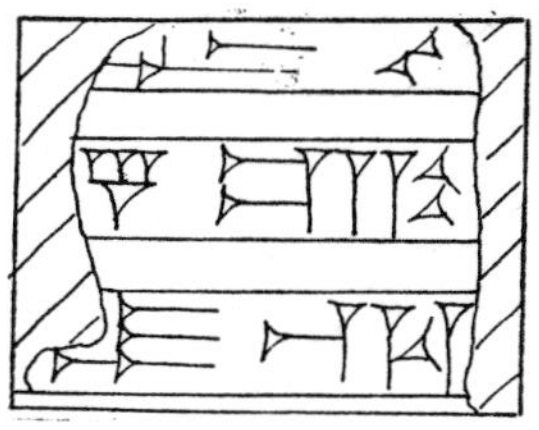
98

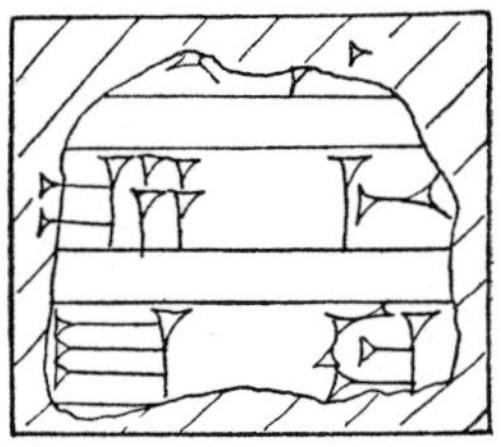
99

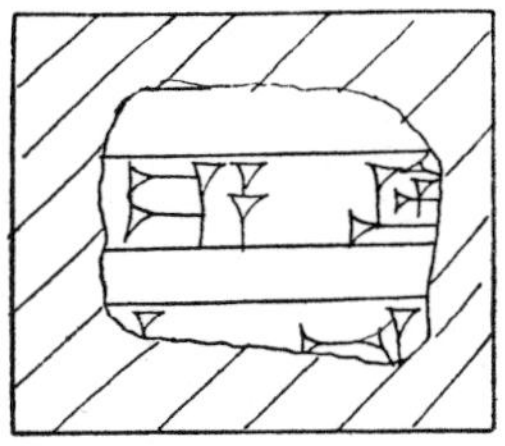
100

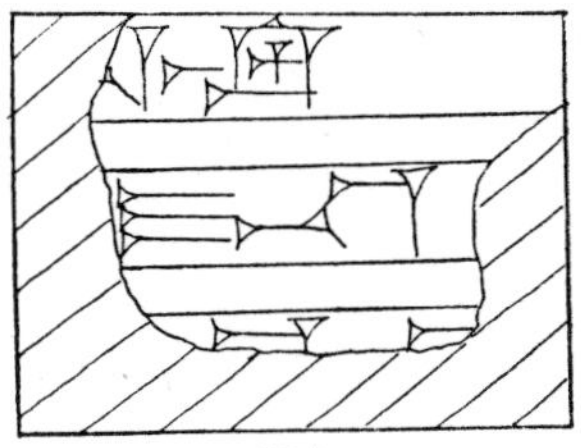
101

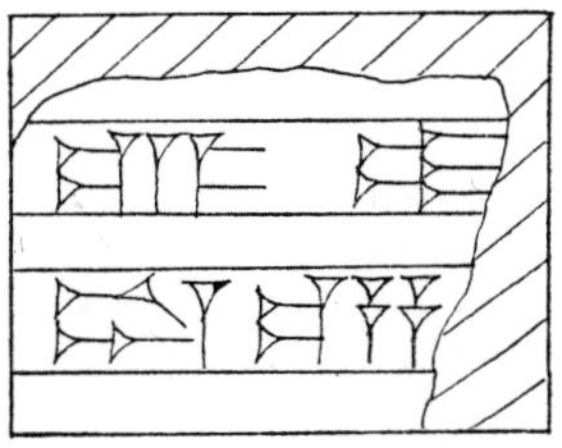
102

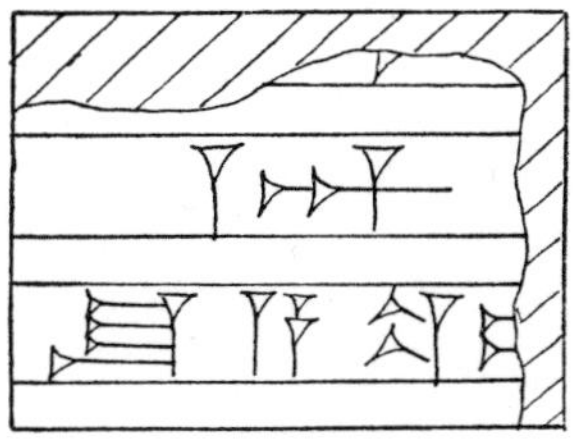
103

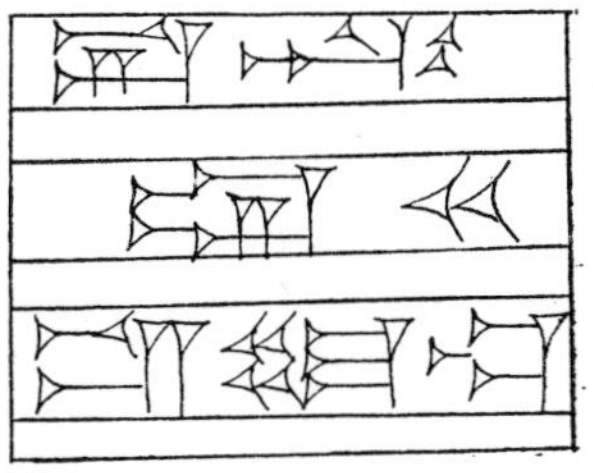
104

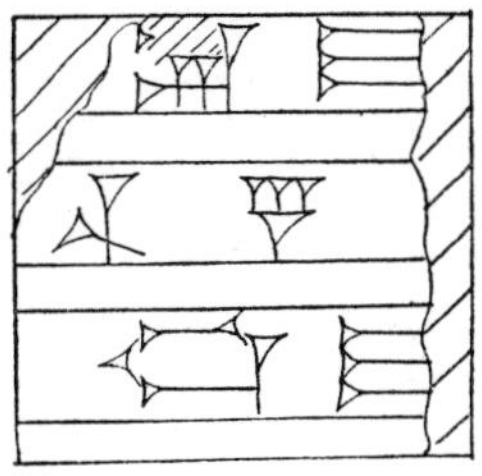
105

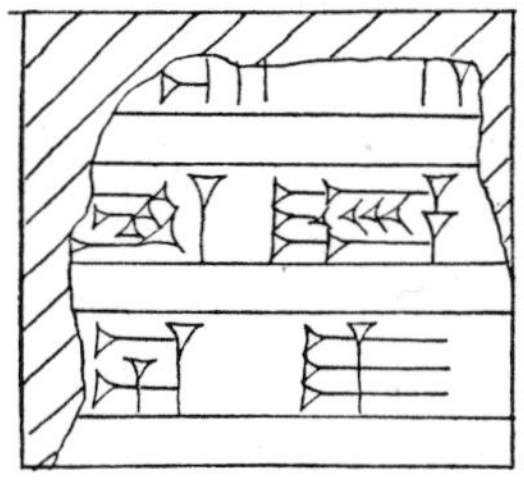
106

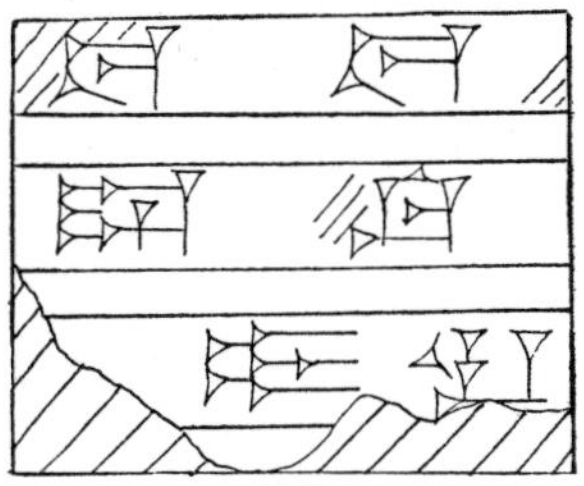
107

Facsimiles. Scale, 1:15

JERWAN INSCRIPTION *D*. PORTIONS FOUND ON RE-USED BLOCKS

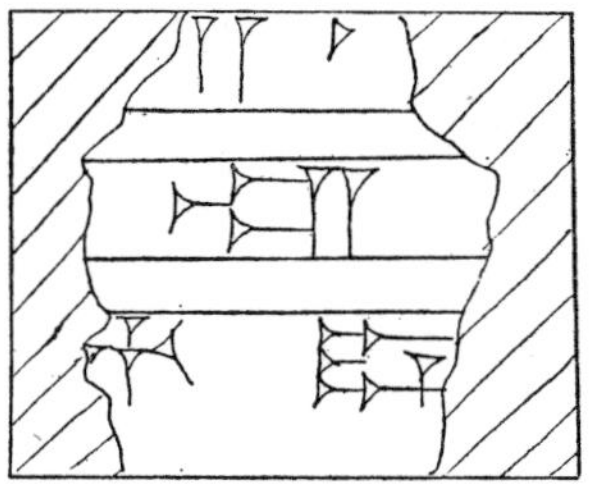

108

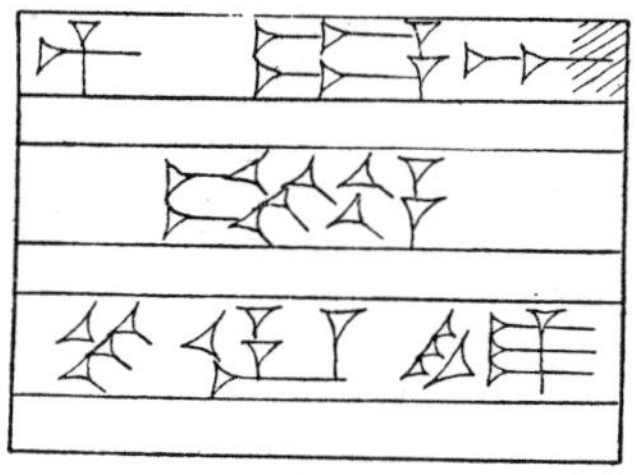

109

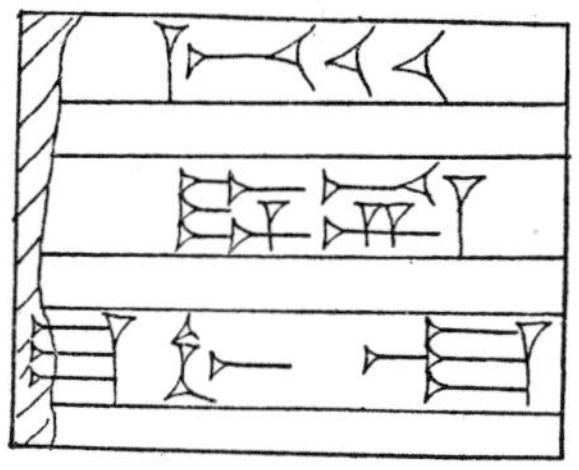

110

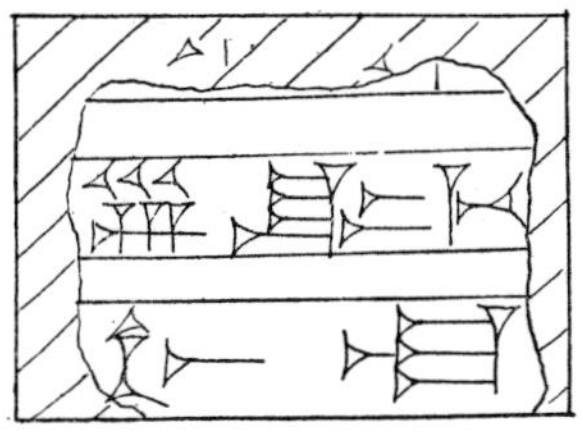

111

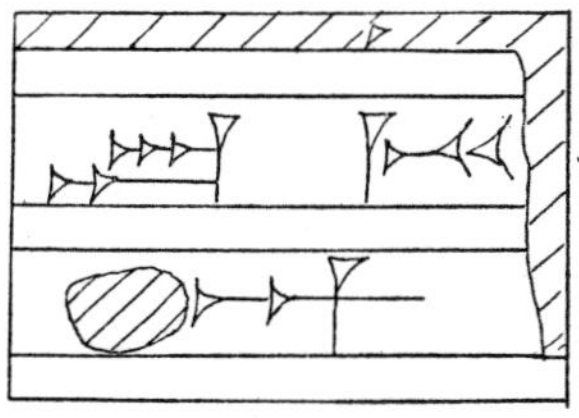

112

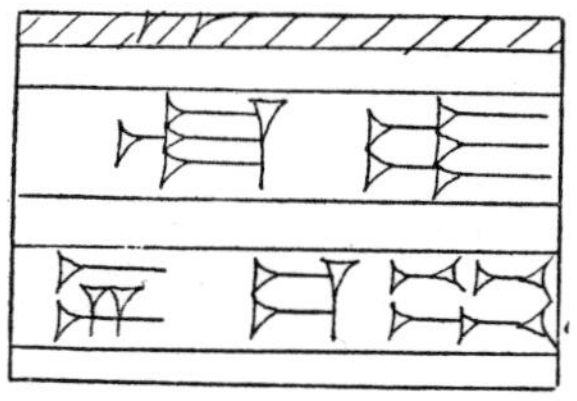

113

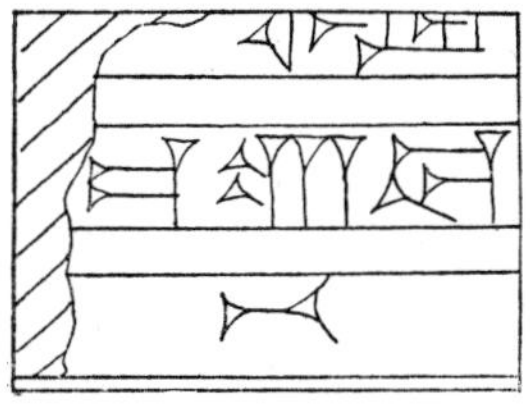

114

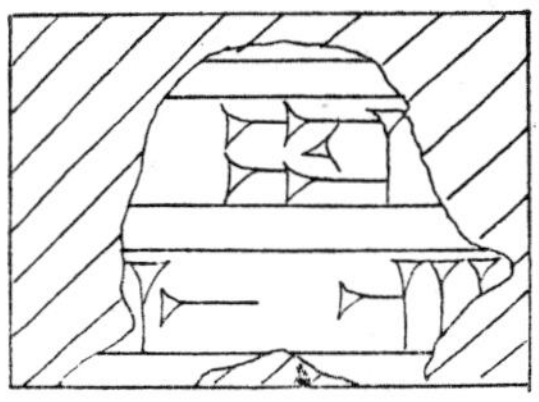

115

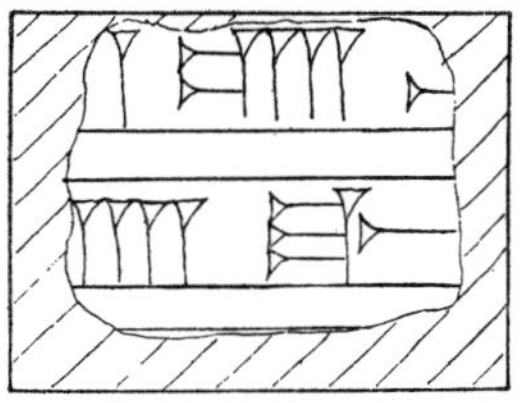

116

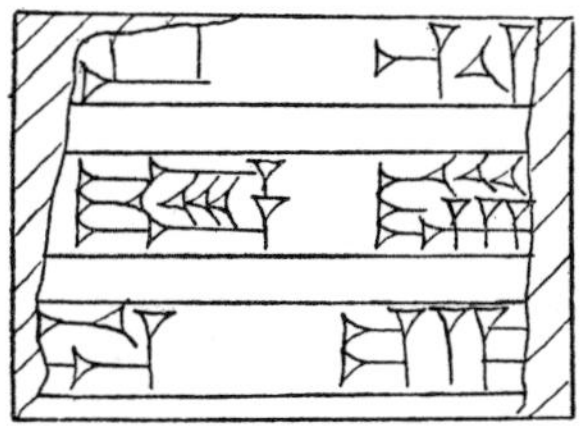

117

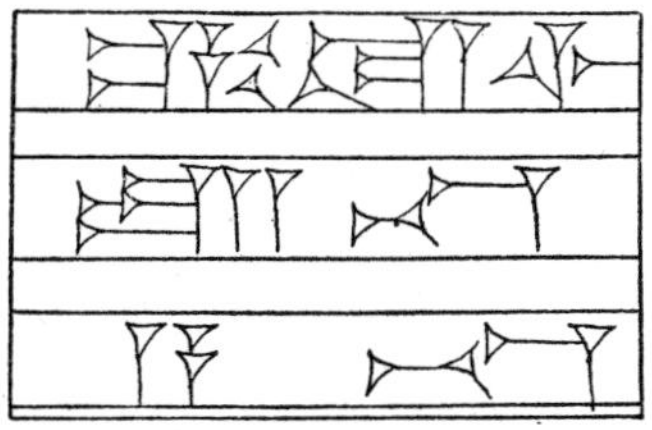

118

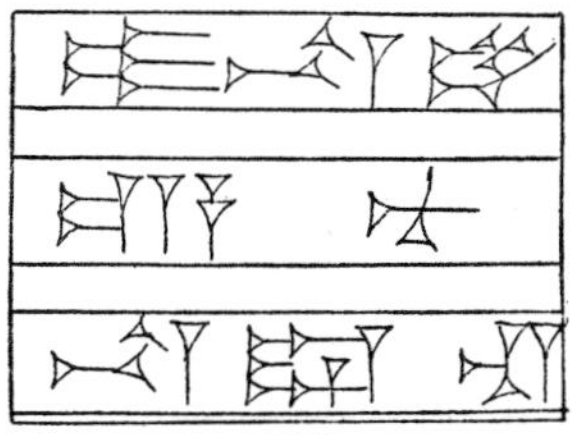

119

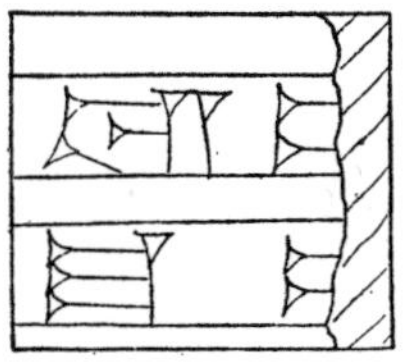

120

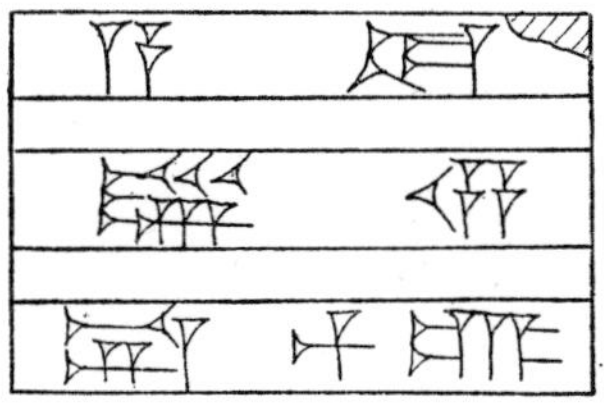

121

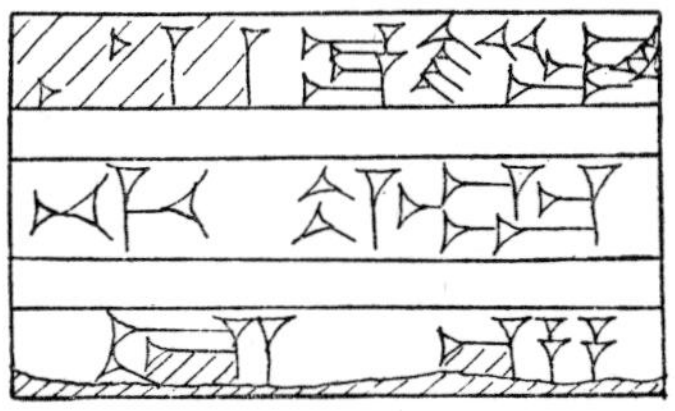

122

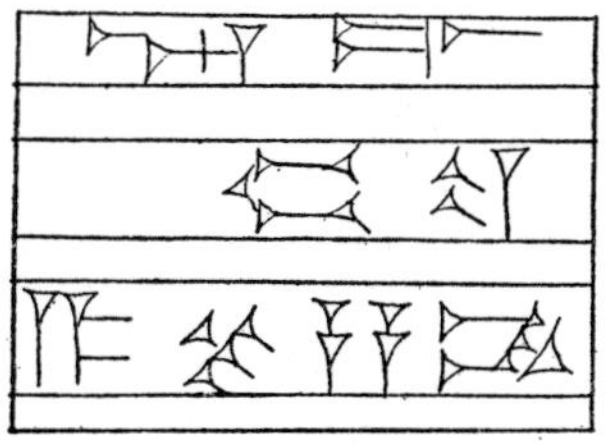

123

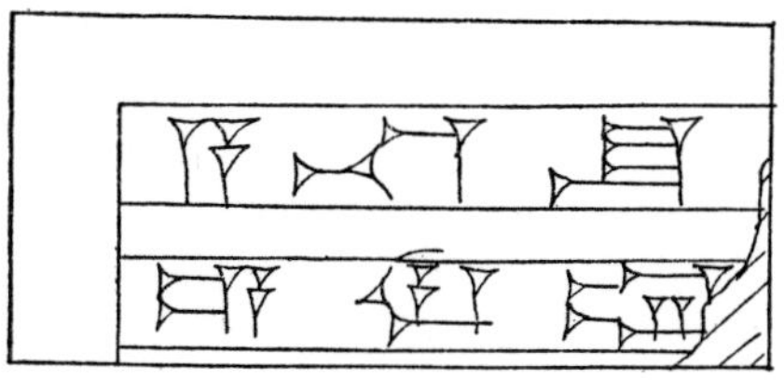

124

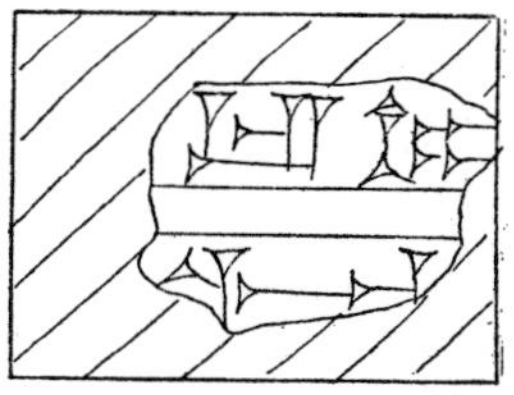

125

Facsimiles. Scale, 1:15

Jerwan inscription *D*. Portions found on re-used blocks

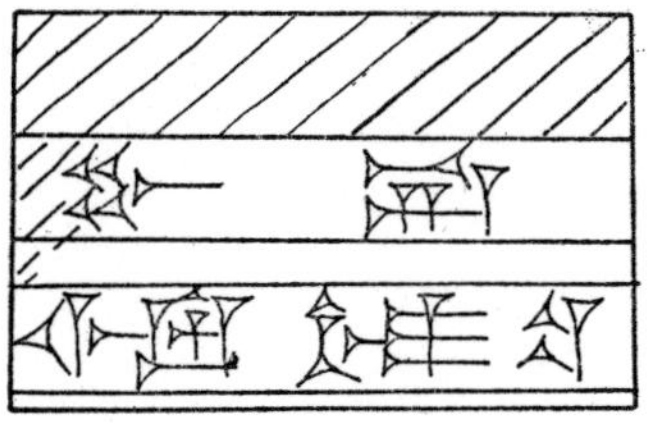
126

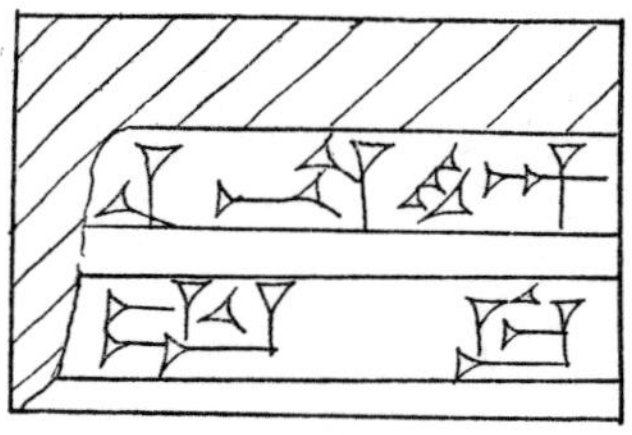
127

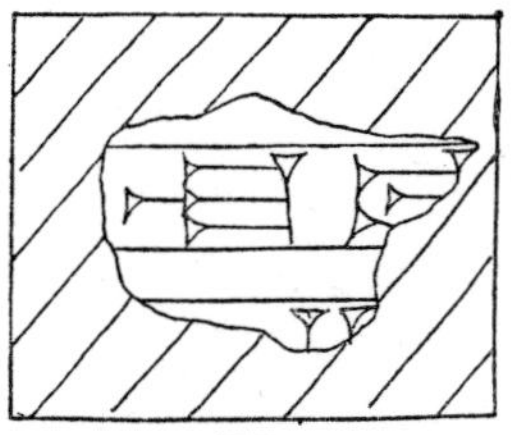
127a

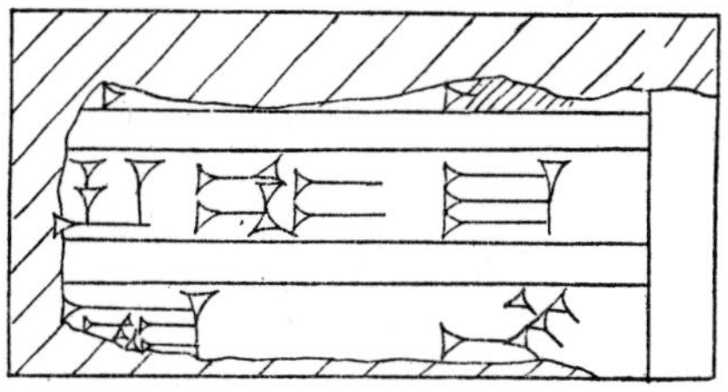
128

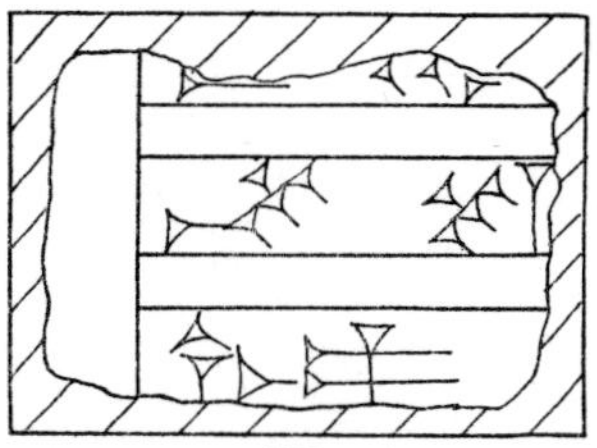
129

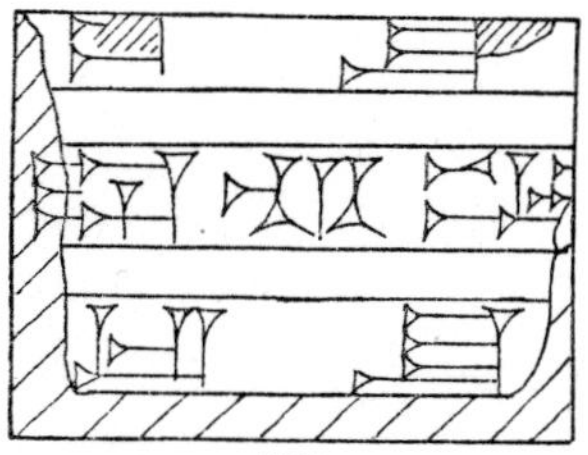
130

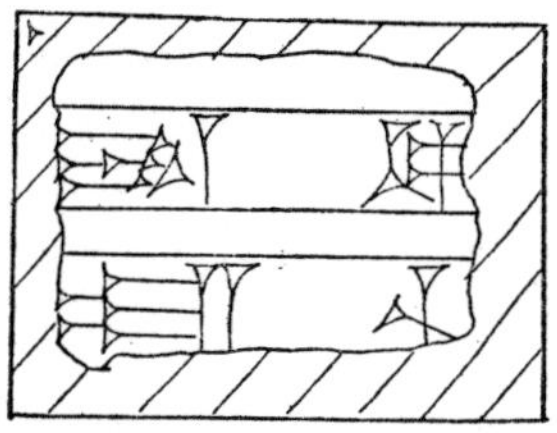
131

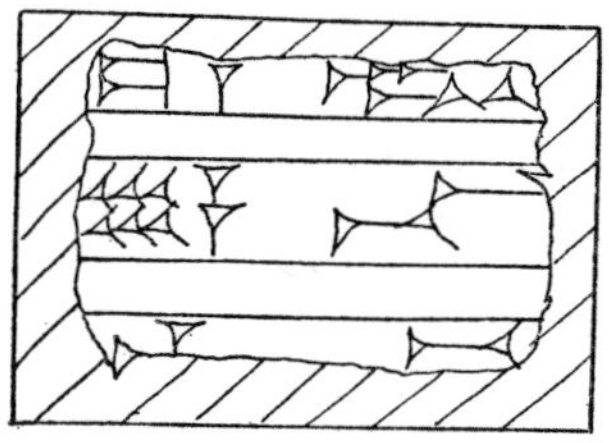
132

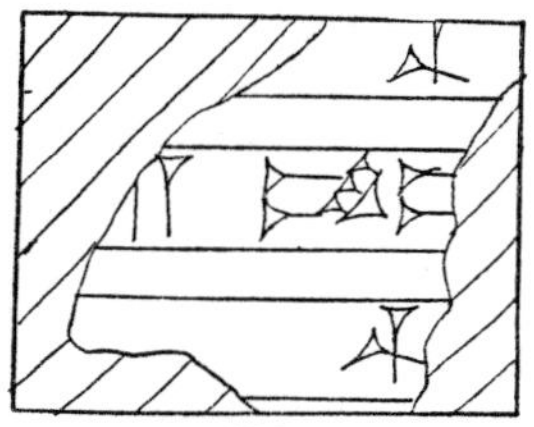
133

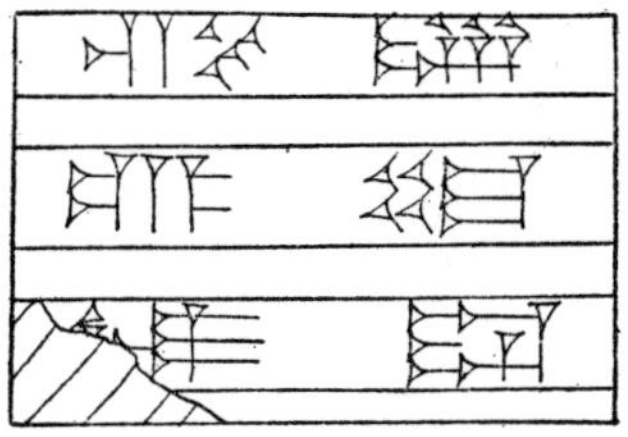
134

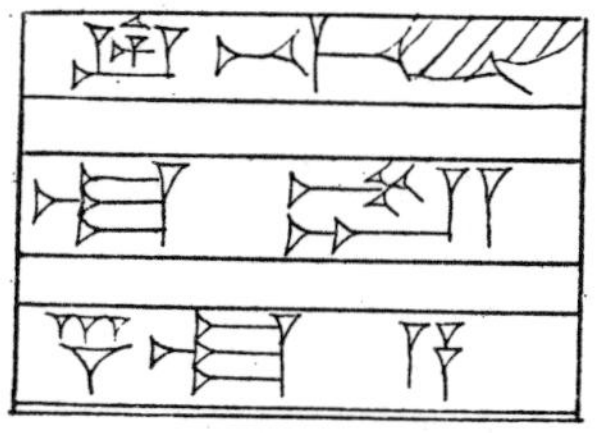
135

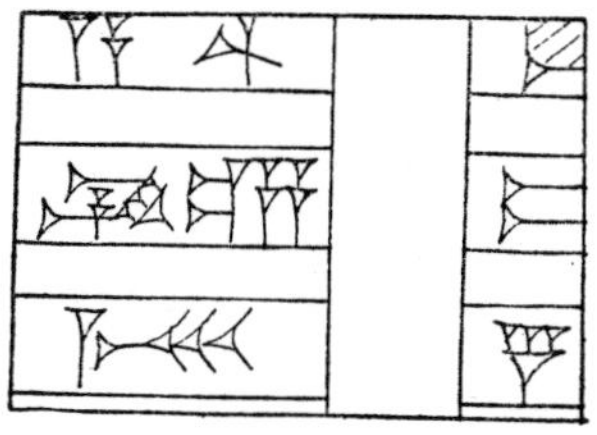
136

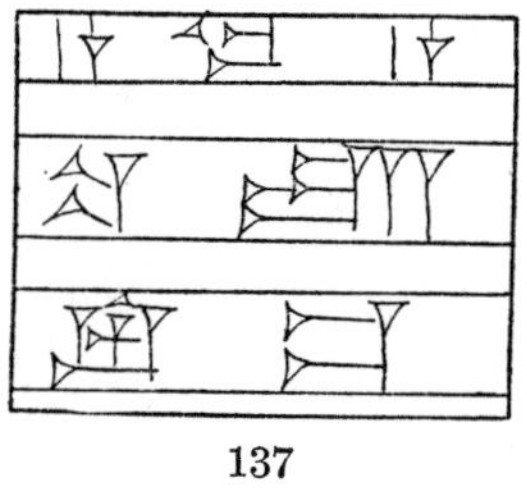
137

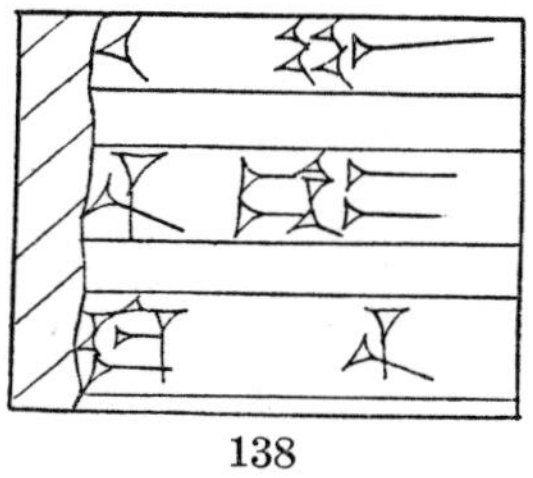
138

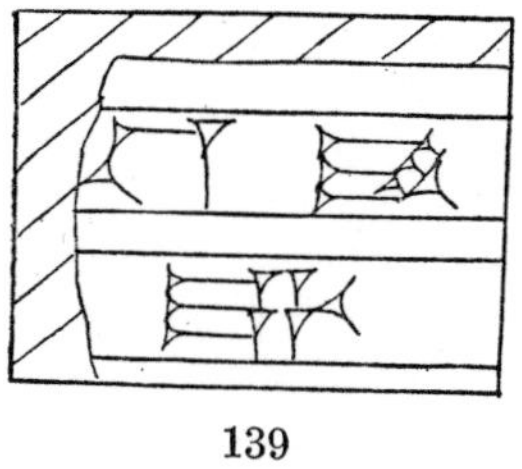
139

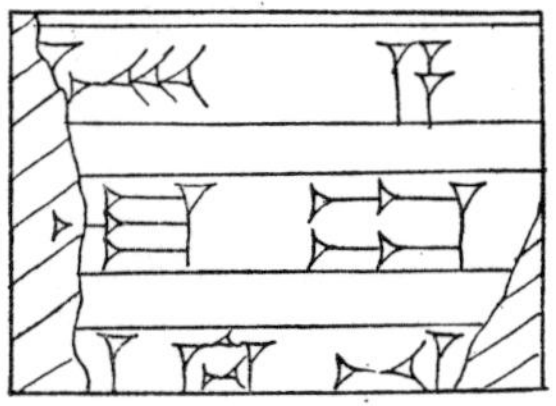
140

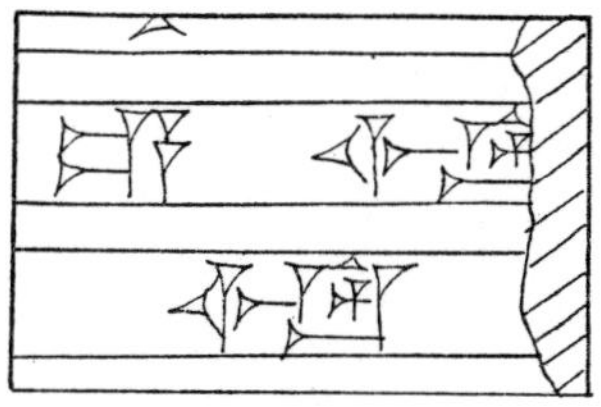
141

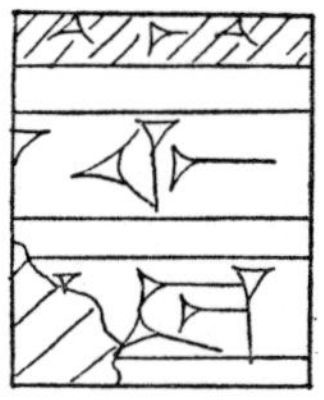
142

Facsimiles. Scale, 1:15

JERWAN INSCRIPTION *D*. PORTIONS FOUND ON RE-USED BLOCKS

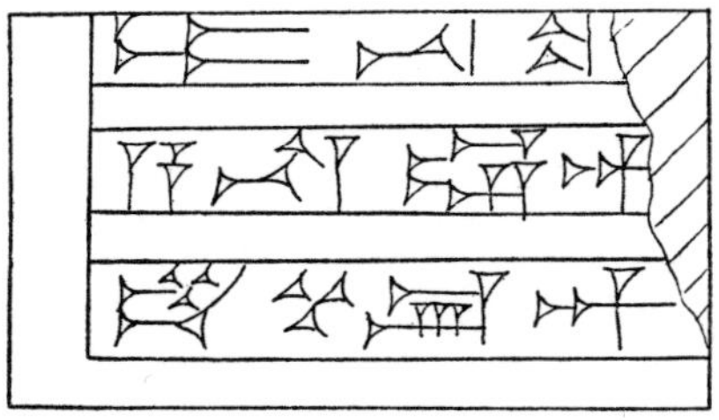
143

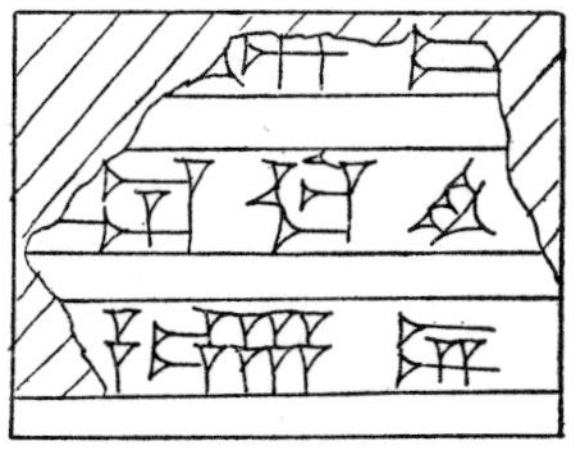
144

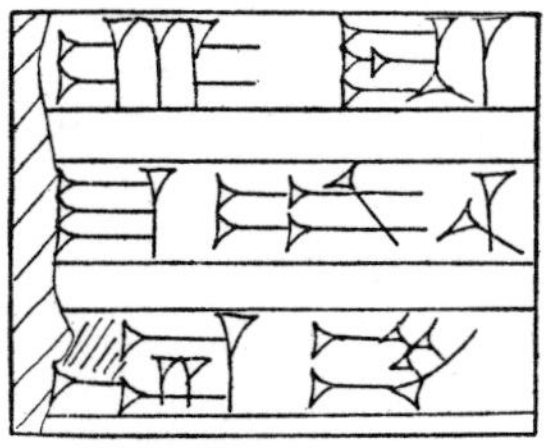
145

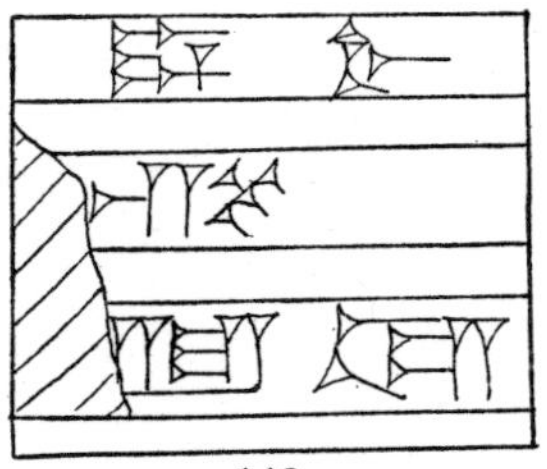
146

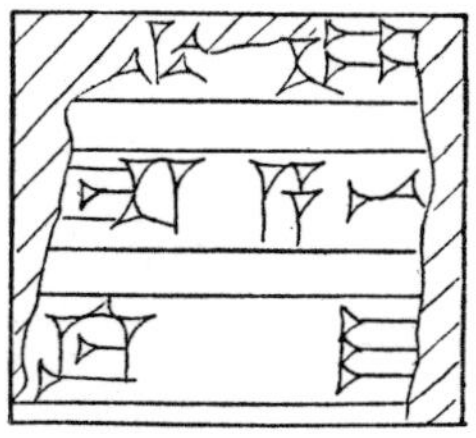
147

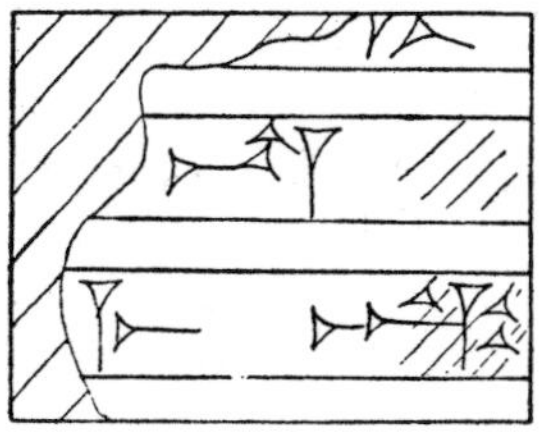
148

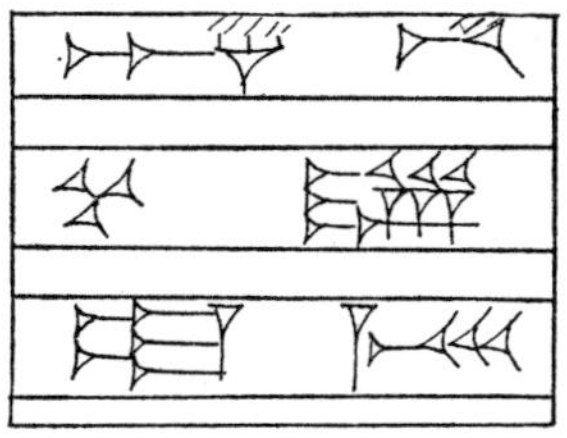
149

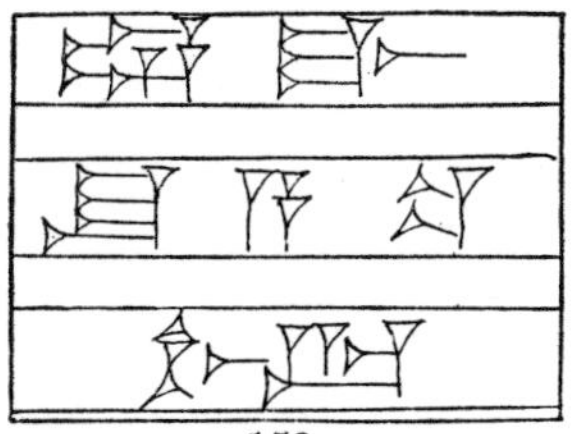
150

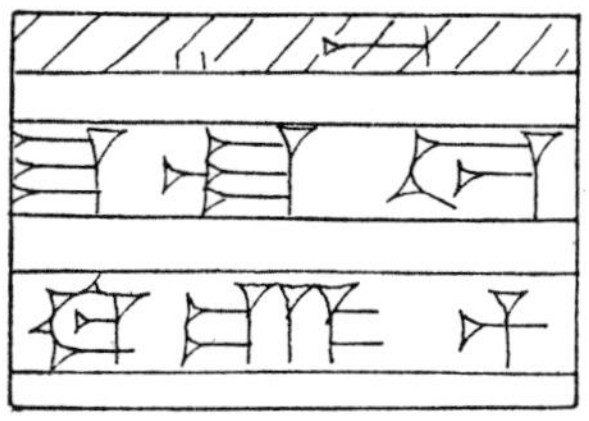
151

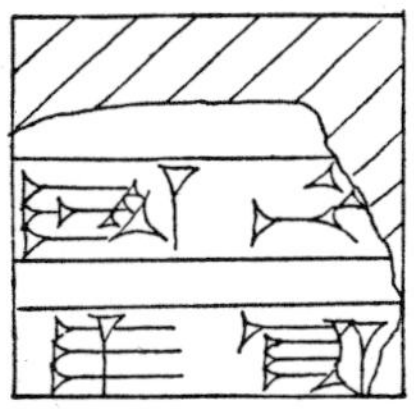
152

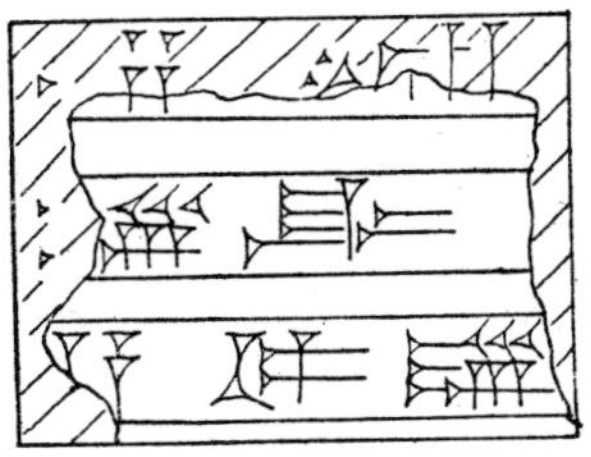
153

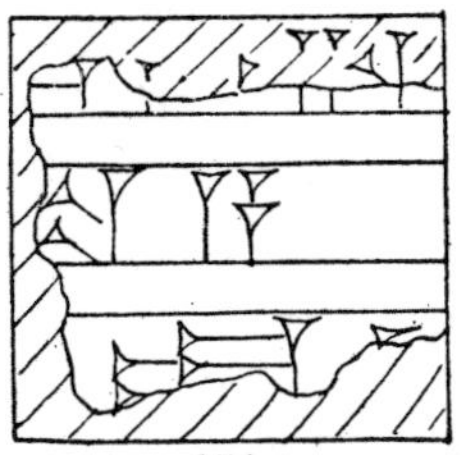
154

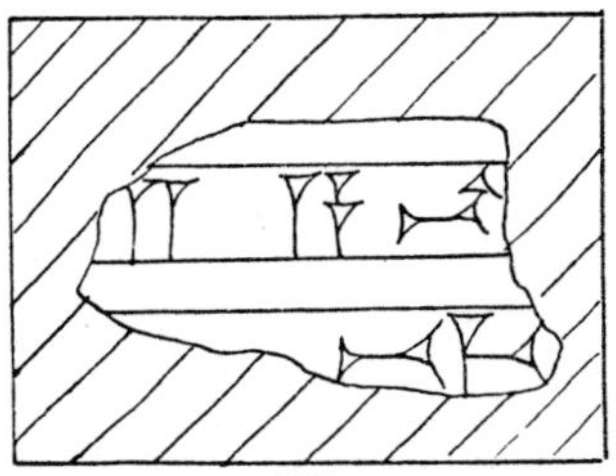
155

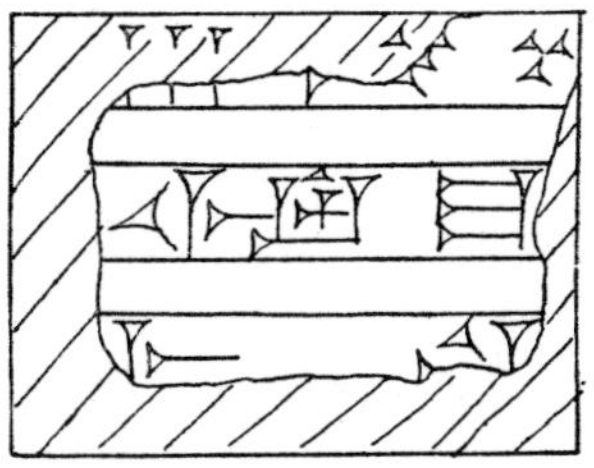
156

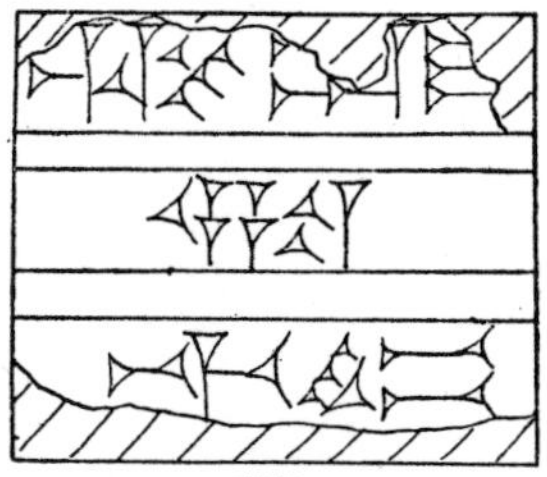
157

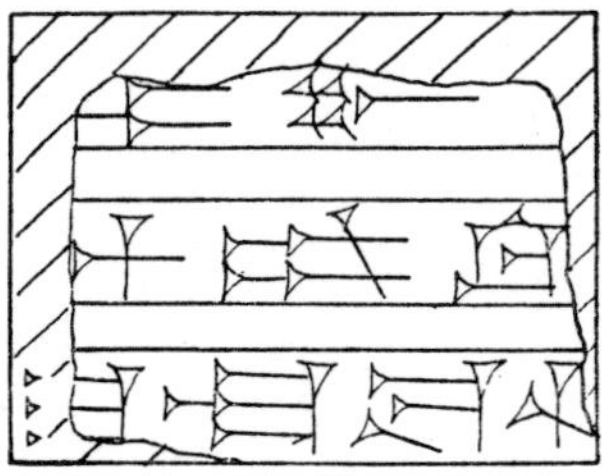
158

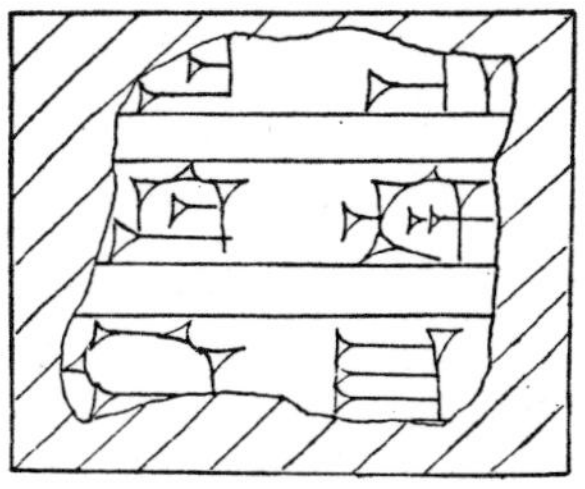
159

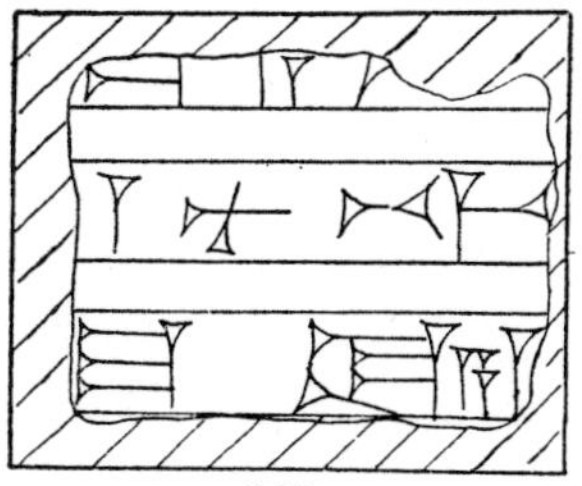
160

Facsimiles. Scale, 1:15

JERWAN INSCRIPTION *D*. PORTIONS FOUND ON RE-USED BLOCKS

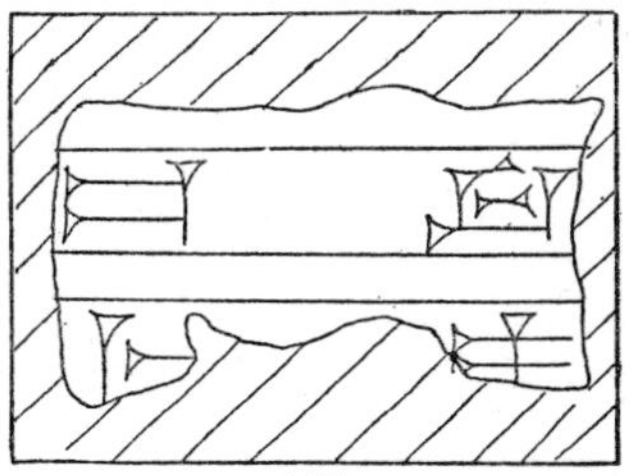
161

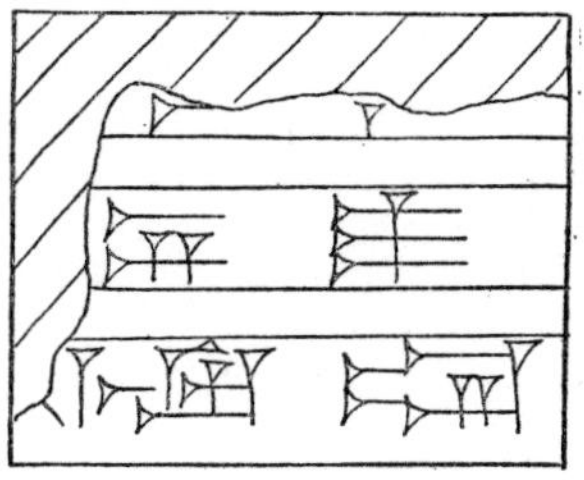
162

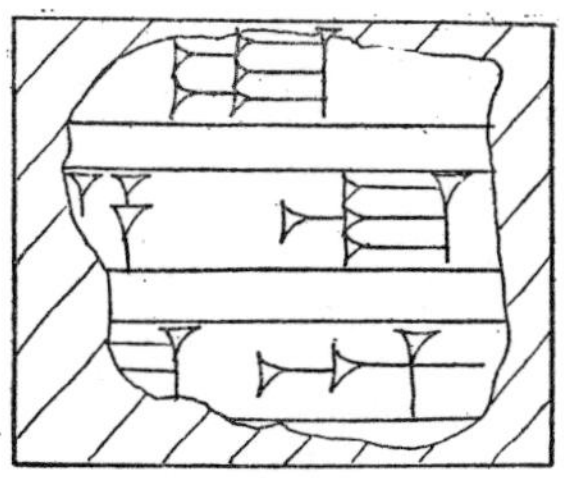
163

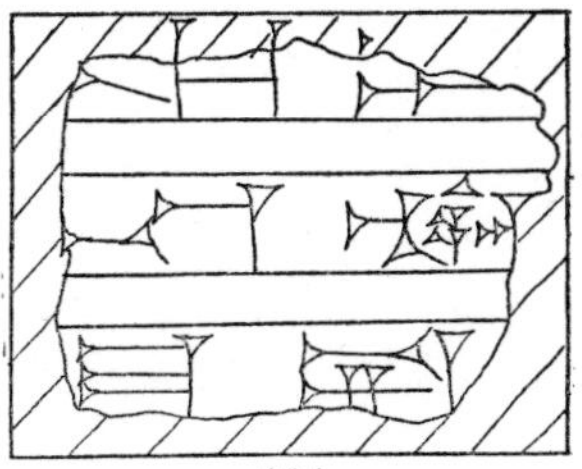
164

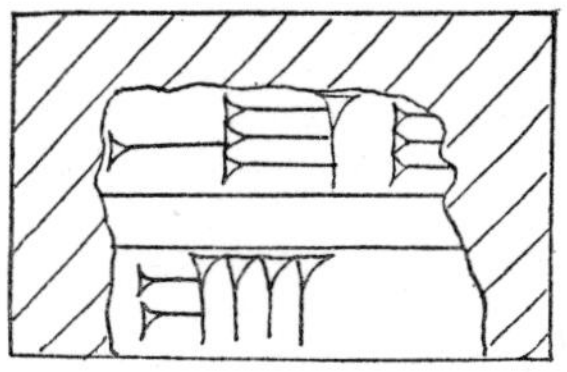
165

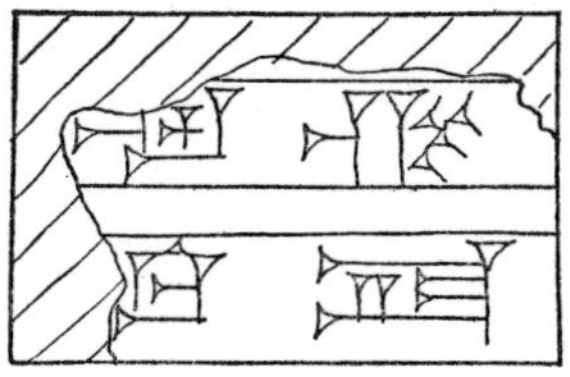
166

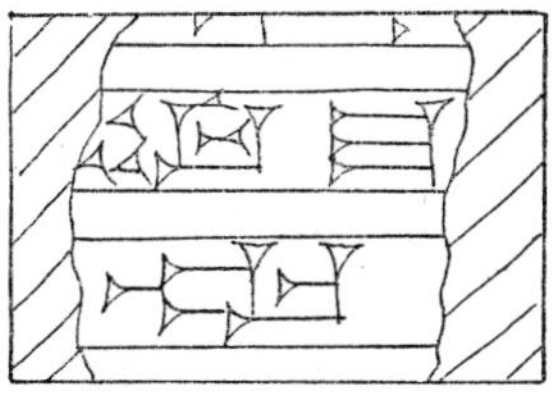
167

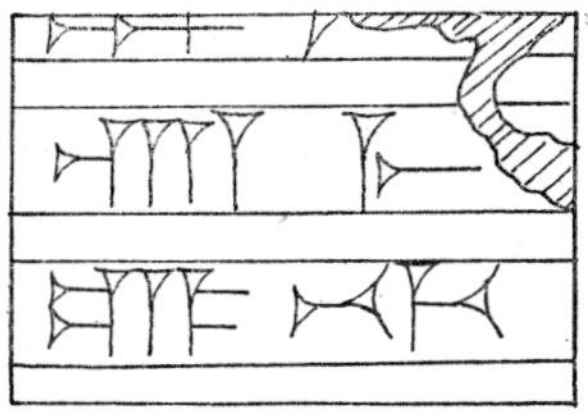
168

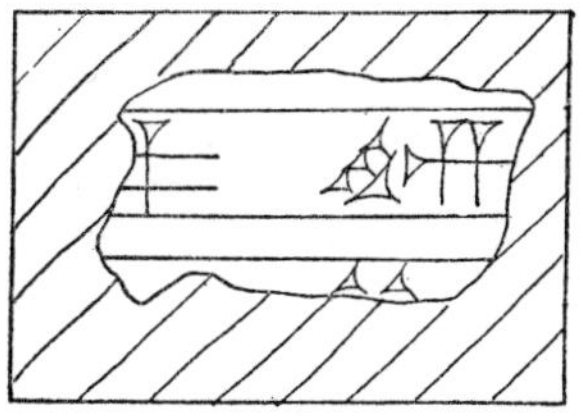
169

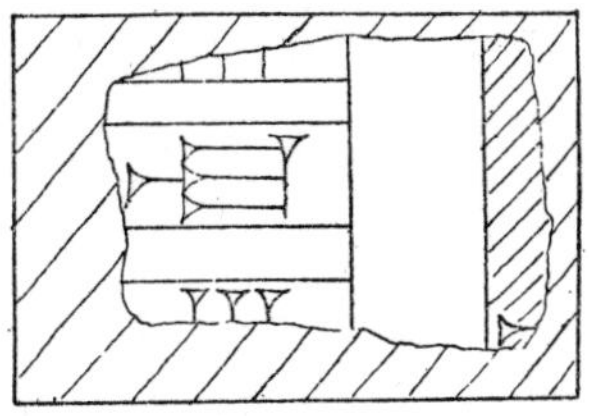
170

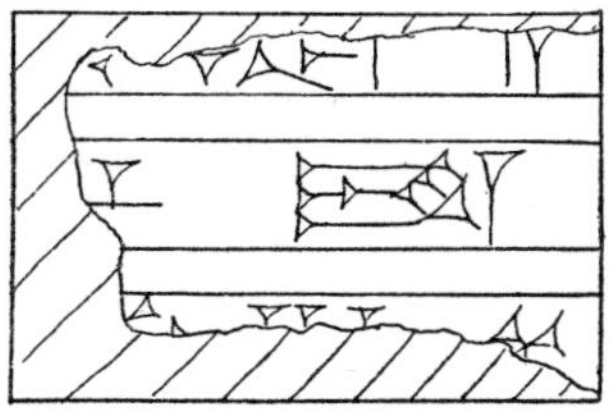
171

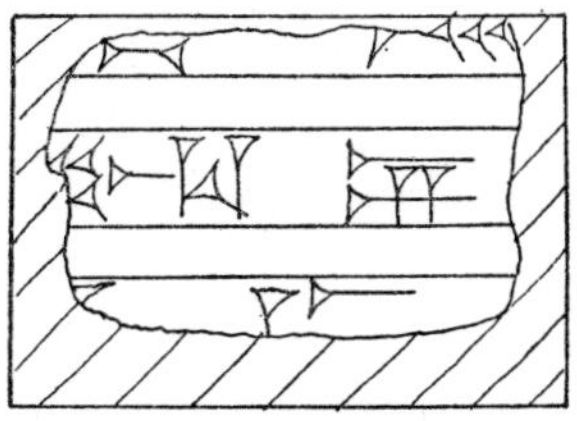
172

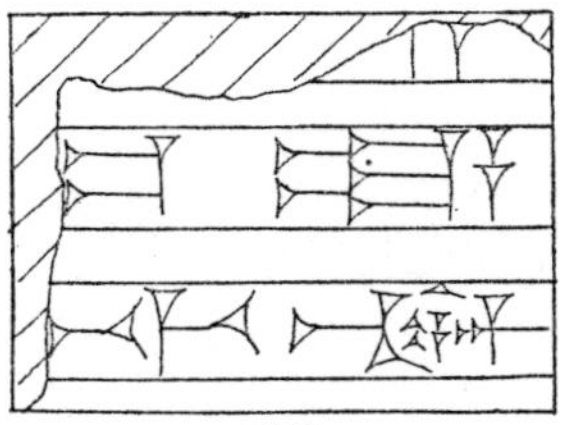
173

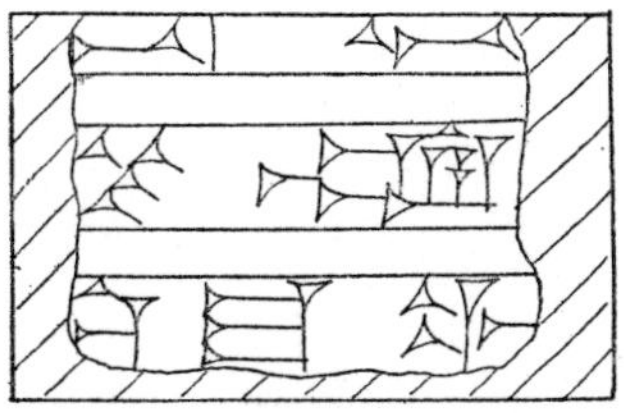
174

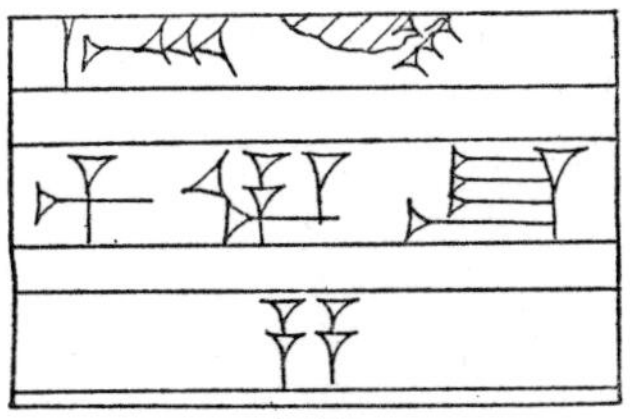
175

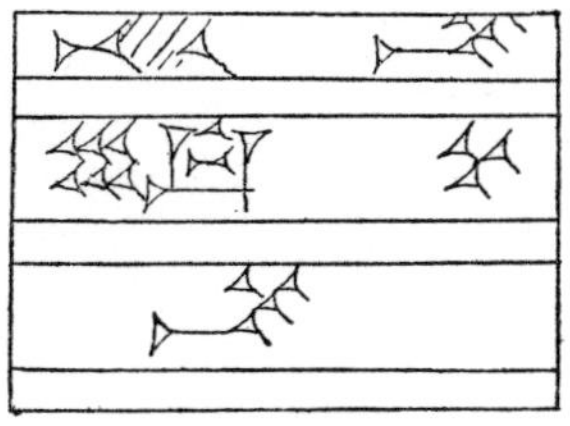
176

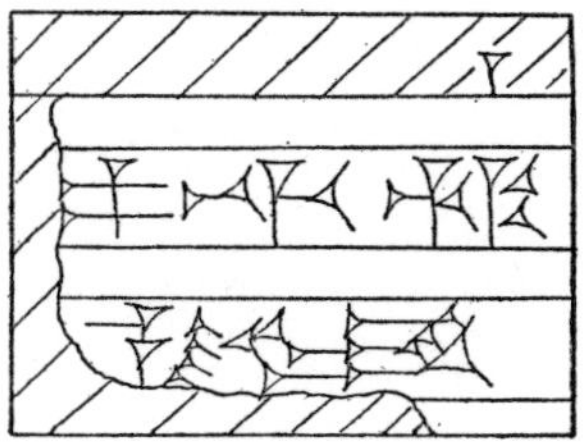
177

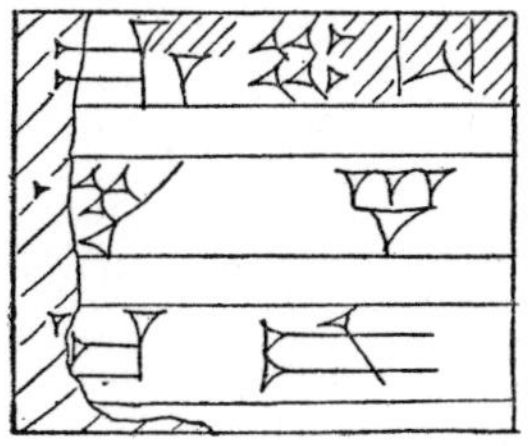
178

Facsimiles. Scale, 1:15

JERWAN INSCRIPTION *D*. PORTIONS FOUND ON RE-USED BLOCKS

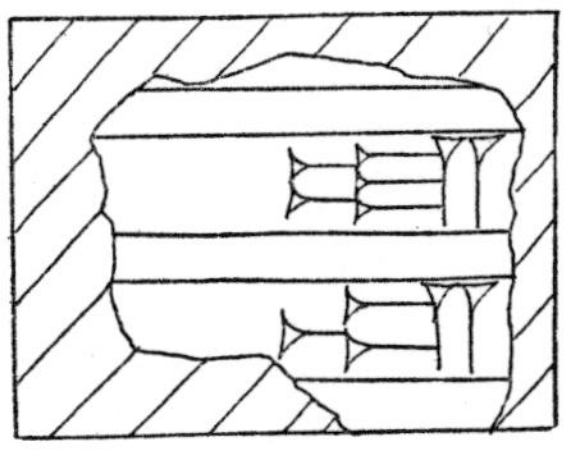
179

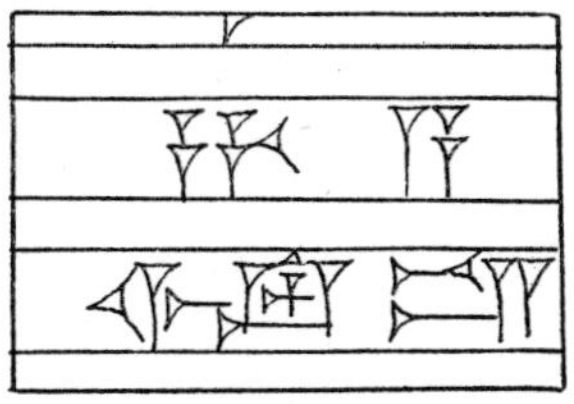
180

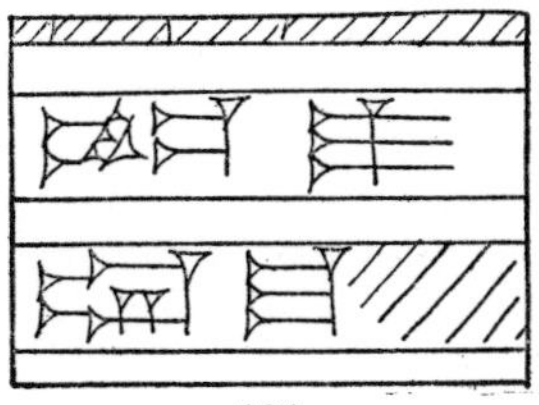
181

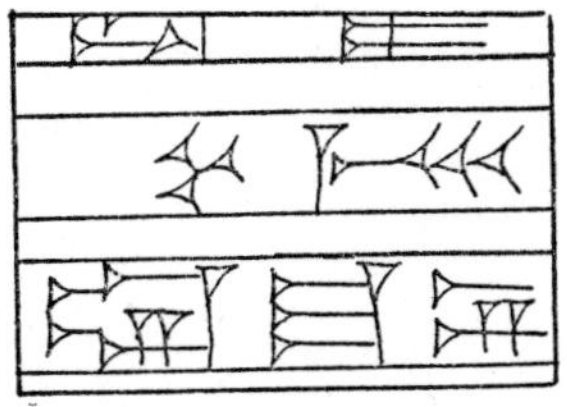
182

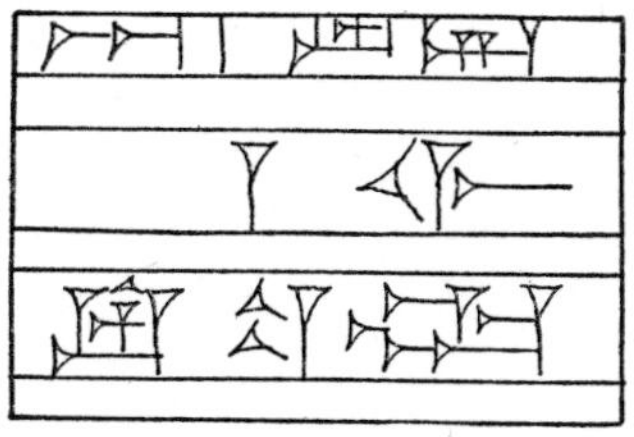
183

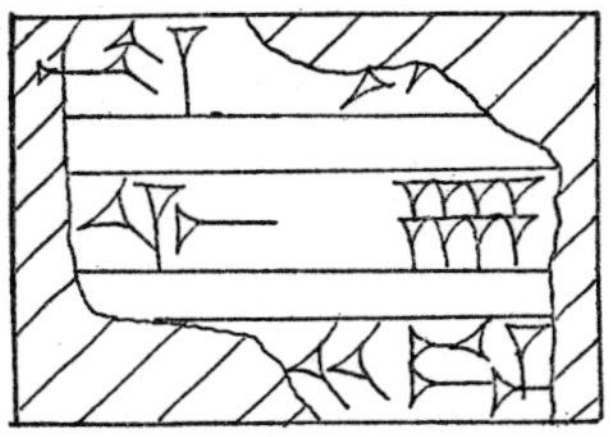
184

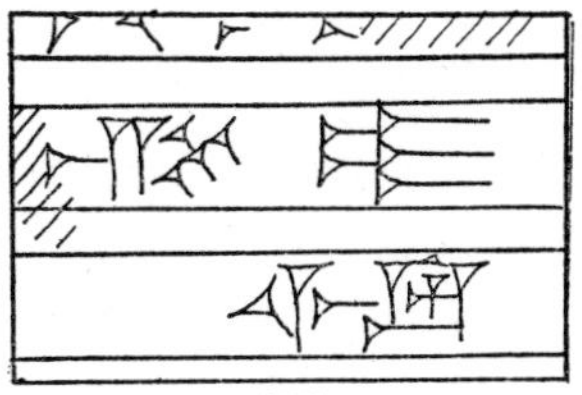
185

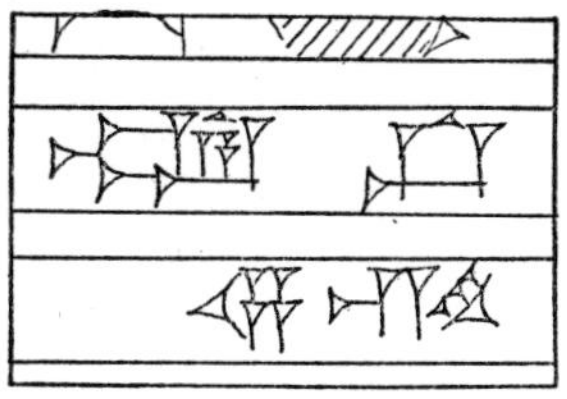
186

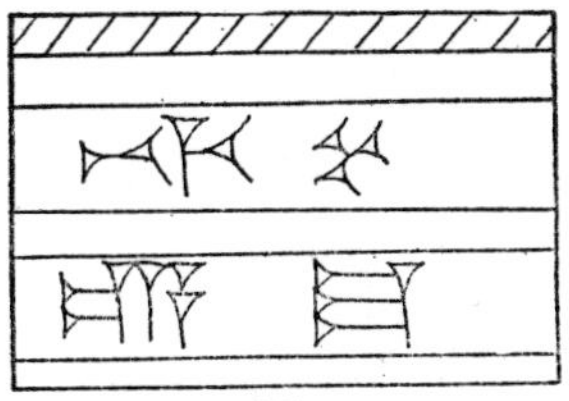
187

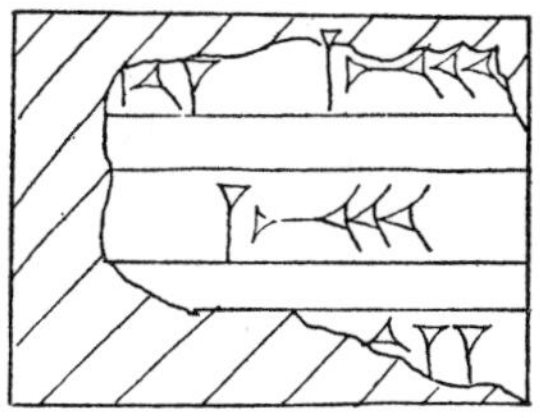
188

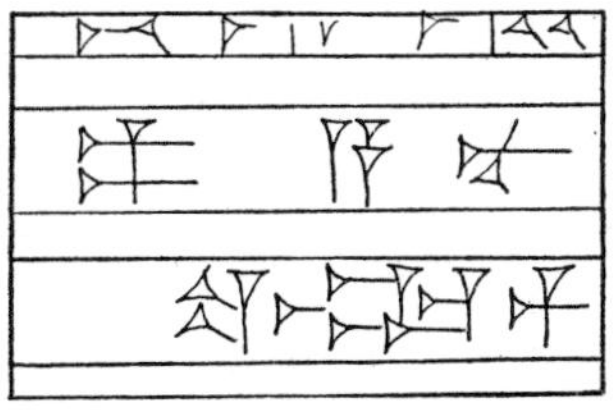
189

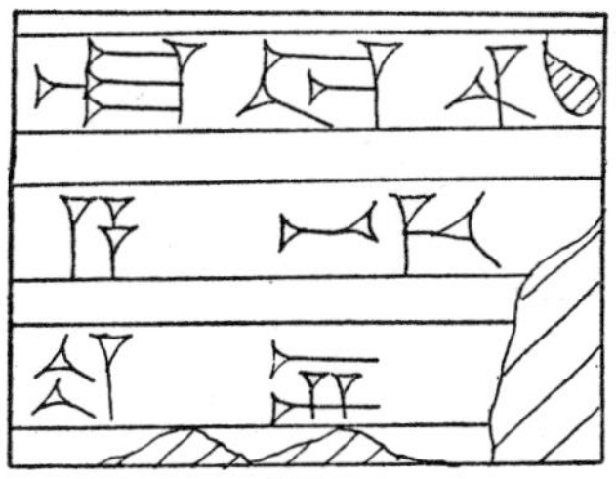
190

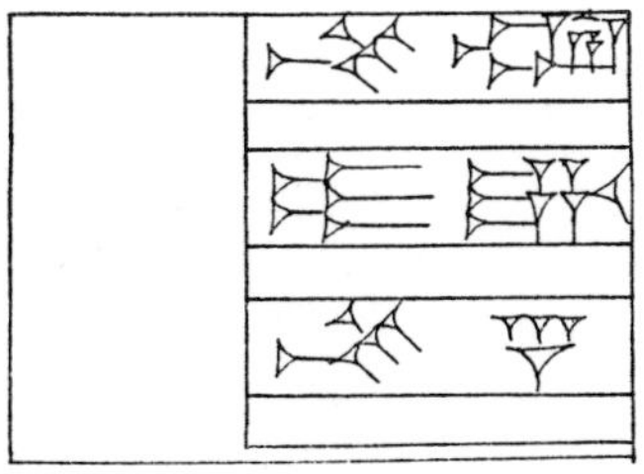
191

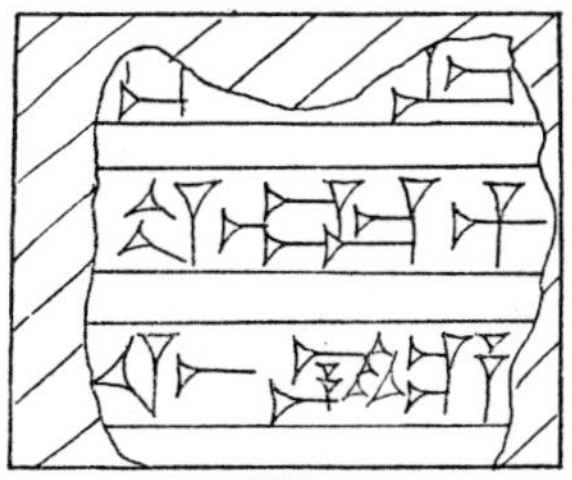
192

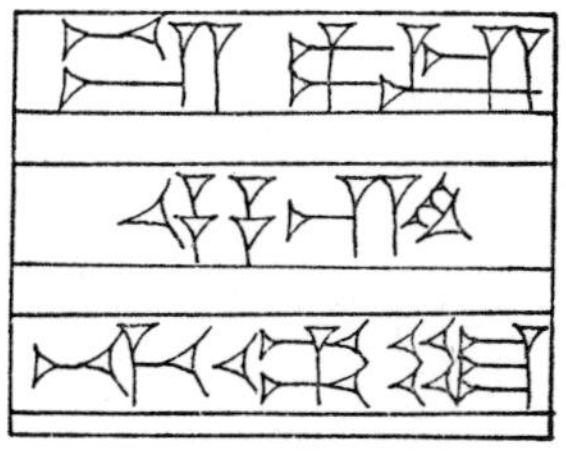
193

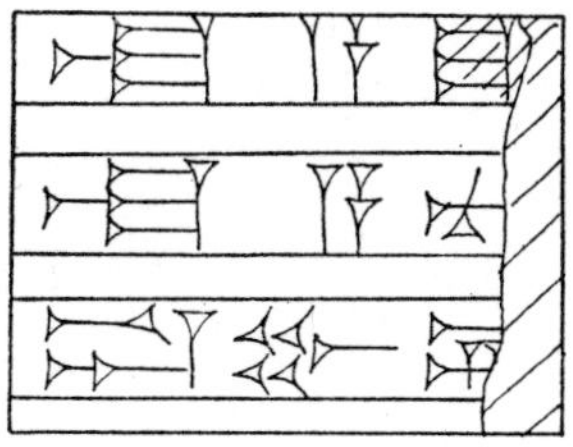
194

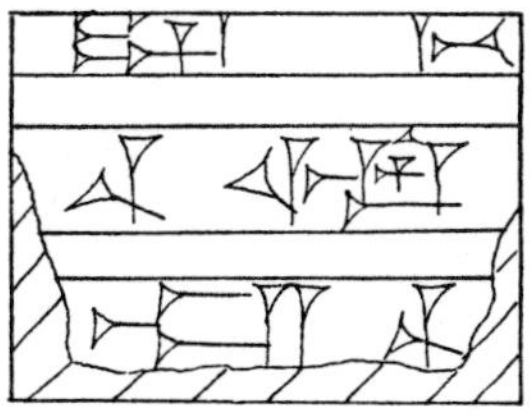
195

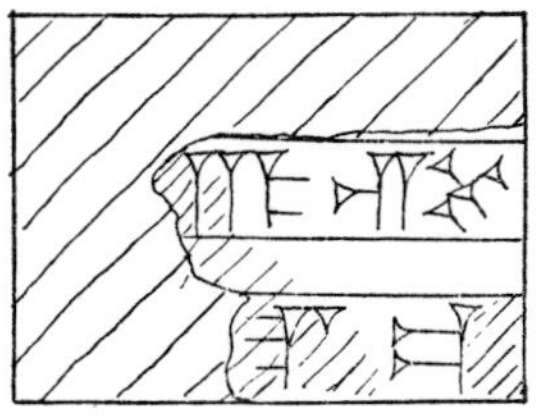
196

Facsimiles. Scale, 1:15

PLATE XXX

JERWAN INSCRIPTION *D*. PORTIONS FOUND ON RE-USED BLOCKS NOW FALLEN

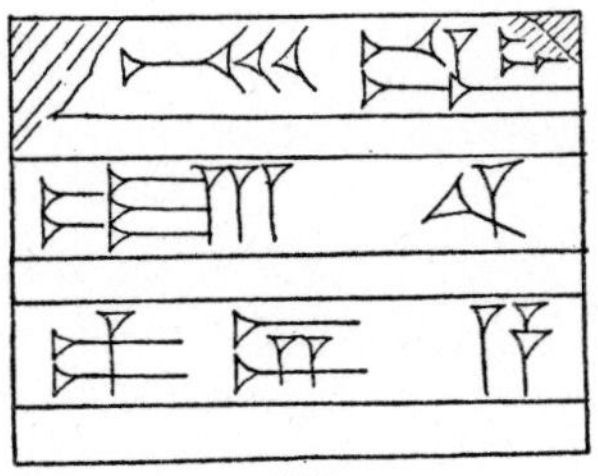
197

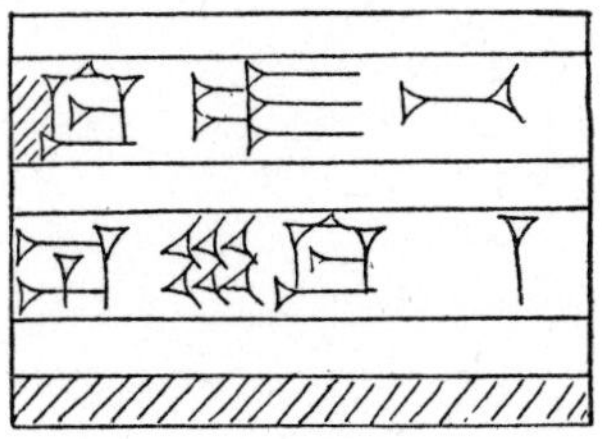
198

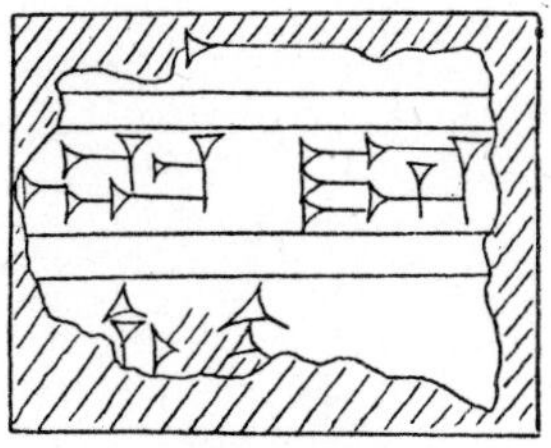
199

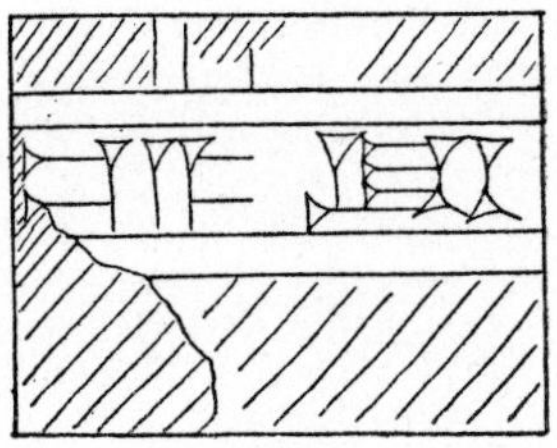
200

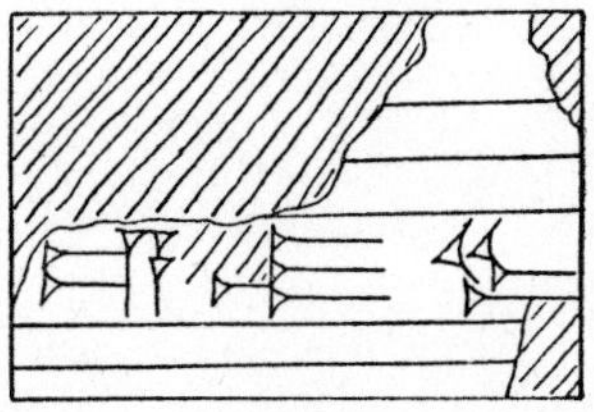
201

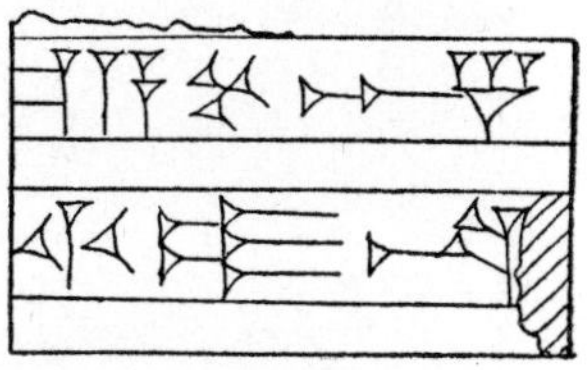
202

Facsimiles. Scale, 1:15

TRACES OF THE BAVIAN-KHOSR CANAL

A.—Stones exposed at Shifshirin

B.—The channel (*A* in Fig. 10) cut into the rocks of the Gomel gorge north of Ḫines, seen from the south before excavation

The Gomel gorge

Dr. Jacobsen, suspended from a cliff, collating an Assyrian inscription

Large panel sculptured in relief on the cliff face (*G* in Fig. 10)

THE GOMEL GORGE. SCULPTURED BLOCK FALLEN, BROKEN, AND PARTIALLY SUBMERGED (*R* IN FIG. 10)

A.—From the east

B.—From the north, with large relief panel (Pl. XXXIII) in background

The canal channel (*A* in Fig. 10) from the east, when excavation had just begun. Steps cut in the rock are seen in center just below the channel (cf. Fig. 11)

A.—Tunnel by which the canal passed through a spur of rock (at *C* in Fig. 10). The masonry of the eastern parapet abuts the rock face (cf. Fig. 11)

B.—Steps cut inside the channel (see Fig. 11, at left). The boy stands on the stone floor of the canal

C–D.—The lion spring (*S* in Fig. 10), from the east